REST API Design Rulebook

Mark Massé

O'REILLY®

Beijing · Cambridge · Farnham · Köln · Sebastopol · Tokyo

REST API Design Rulebook
by Mark Massé

Copyright © 2012 Mark Massé. All rights reserved.
Printed in the United States of America.

Published by O'Reilly Media, Inc., 1005 Gravenstein Highway North, Sebastopol, CA 95472.

O'Reilly books may be purchased for educational, business, or sales promotional use. Online editions are also available for most titles (*http://my.safaribooksonline.com*). For more information, contact our corporate/institutional sales department: (800) 998-9938 or *corporate@oreilly.com*.

Editor: Simon St. Laurent	**Cover Designer:** Karen Montgomery
Production Editor: Kristen Borg	**Interior Designer:** David Futato
Proofreader: O'Reilly Production Services	**Illustrator:** Robert Romano

Revision History for the First Edition:

2011-10-17   First release

See *http://oreilly.com/catalog/errata.csp?isbn=9781449310509* for release details.

ISBN: 978-1-449-31050-9

[LSI]

1318535719

For my amazing dad, Robert P. Massé, who is the author of books on subjects ranging from the "Nature of Physical Fields and Forces" to a mysterious "Ghost Nose" that rides a big wheel.

Dad, thanks for giving me my very first O'Reilly book and for teaching me to never stop learning.

Table of Contents

Preface ix

1. **Introduction** 1
   Hello World Wide Web   1
   Web Architecture   2
      Client–Server   3
      Uniform Interface   3
      Layered System   4
      Cache   4
      Stateless   4
      Code-On-Demand   4
   Web Standards   5
   REST   5
   REST APIs   5
   REST API Design   6
      Rules   6
      WRML   7
   Recap   7

2. **Identifier Design with URIs** 11
   URIs   11
   URI Format   11
      Rule: Forward slash separator (/) must be used to indicate a hierarchical
      relationship   12
      Rule: A trailing forward slash (/) should not be included in URIs   12
      Rule: Hyphens (-) should be used to improve the readability of URIs   12
      Rule: Underscores (_) should not be used in URIs   12
      Rule: Lowercase letters should be preferred in URI paths   13
      Rule: File extensions should not be included in URIs   13
   URI Authority Design   14
      Rule: Consistent subdomain names should be used for your APIs   14

      Rule: Consistent subdomain names should be used for your client de-
        veloper portal   14
    Resource Modeling   14
    Resource Archetypes   15
      Document   15
      Collection   15
      Store   16
      Controller   16
    URI Path Design   16
      Rule: A singular noun should be used for document names   17
      Rule: A plural noun should be used for collection names   17
      Rule: A plural noun should be used for store names   17
      Rule: A verb or verb phrase should be used for controller names   17
      Rule: Variable path segments may be substituted with identity-based
        values   18
      Rule: CRUD function names should not be used in URIs   18
    URI Query Design   19
      Rule: The query component of a URI may be used to filter collections
        or stores   19
      Rule: The query component of a URI should be used to paginate col-
        lection or store results   20
    Recap   20

3. Interaction Design with HTTP **23**
    HTTP/1.1   23
    Request Methods   23
      Rule: GET and POST must not be used to tunnel other request methods   24
      Rule: GET must be used to retrieve a representation of a resource   24
      Rule: HEAD should be used to retrieve response headers   25
      Rule: PUT must be used to both insert and update a stored resource   25
      Rule: PUT must be used to update mutable resources   26
      Rule: POST must be used to create a new resource in a collection   26
      Rule: POST must be used to execute controllers   26
      Rule: DELETE must be used to remove a resource from its parent   27
      Rule: OPTIONS should be used to retrieve metadata that describes a
        resource's available interactions   27
    Response Status Codes   28
      Rule: 200 ("OK") should be used to indicate nonspecific success   28
      Rule: 200 ("OK") must not be used to communicate errors in the re-
        sponse body   28
      Rule: 201 ("Created") must be used to indicate successful resource cre-
        ation   28

Rule: 202 ("Accepted") must be used to indicate successful start of an asynchronous action 29

Rule: 204 ("No Content") should be used when the response body is intentionally empty 29

Rule: 301 ("Moved Permanently") should be used to relocate resources 29

Rule: 302 ("Found") should not be used 29

Rule: 303 ("See Other") should be used to refer the client to a different URI 30

Rule: 304 ("Not Modified") should be used to preserve bandwidth 30

Rule: 307 ("Temporary Redirect") should be used to tell clients to re-submit the request to another URI 30

Rule: 400 ("Bad Request") may be used to indicate nonspecific failure 30

Rule: 401 ("Unauthorized") must be used when there is a problem with the client's credentials 31

Rule: 403 ("Forbidden") should be used to forbid access regardless of authorization state 31

Rule: 404 ("Not Found") must be used when a client's URI cannot be mapped to a resource 31

Rule: 405 ("Method Not Allowed") must be used when the HTTP method is not supported 31

Rule: 406 ("Not Acceptable") must be used when the requested media type cannot be served 32

Rule: 409 ("Conflict") should be used to indicate a violation of resource state 32

Rule: 412 ("Precondition Failed") should be used to support conditional operations 32

Rule: 415 ("Unsupported Media Type") must be used when the media type of a request's payload cannot be processed 32

Rule: 500 ("Internal Server Error") should be used to indicate API malfunction 32

Recap 33

4. Metadata Design 35

HTTP Headers 35

Rule: Content-Type must be used 35

Rule: Content-Length should be used 35

Rule: Last-Modified should be used in responses 35

Rule: ETag should be used in responses 36

Rule: Stores must support conditional PUT requests 36

Rule: Location must be used to specify the URI of a newly created resource 37

Rule: Cache-Control, Expires, and Date response headers should be used to encourage caching 37

Rule: Cache-Control, Expires, and Pragma response headers may be
used to discourage caching   38
Rule: Caching should be encouraged   38
Rule: Expiration caching headers should be used with 200 ("OK") re-
sponses   38
Rule: Expiration caching headers may optionally be used with 3xx and
4xx responses   38
Rule: Custom HTTP headers must not be used to change the behavior
of HTTP methods   38
Media Types   39
Media Type Syntax   39
Registered Media Types   39
Vendor-Specific Media Types   40
Media Type Design   41
Rule: Application-specific media types should be used   41
Rule: Media type negotiation should be supported when multiple rep-
resentations are available   43
Rule: Media type selection using a query parameter may be supported 44
Recap   44

5. **Representation Design** **47**
Message Body Format   47
Rule: JSON should be supported for resource representation   47
Rule: JSON must be well-formed   48
Rule: XML and other formats may optionally be used for resource rep-
resentation   48
Rule: Additional envelopes must not be created   49
Hypermedia Representation   49
Rule: A consistent form should be used to represent links   49
Rule: A consistent form should be used to represent link relations 52
Rule: A consistent form should be used to advertise links   53
Rule: A self link should be included in response message body repre-
sentations   54
Rule: Minimize the number of advertised "entry point" API URIs   54
Rule: Links should be used to advertise a resource's available actions in
a state-sensitive manner   55
Media Type Representation   56
Rule: A consistent form should be used to represent media type formats 56
Rule: A consistent form should be used to represent media type schemas 59
Error Representation   68
Rule: A consistent form should be used to represent errors   68
Rule: A consistent form should be used to represent error responses 69

Rule: Consistent error types should be used for common error conditions   70
Recap   70

6. **Client Concerns** **71**
Introduction   71
Versioning   71
Rule: New URIs should be used to introduce new concepts   71
Rule: Schemas should be used to manage representational form versions 72
Rule: Entity tags should be used to manage representational state versions   72
Security   72
Rule: OAuth may be used to protect resources   72
Rule: API management solutions may be used to protect resources   73
Response Representation Composition   73
Rule: The query component of a URI should be used to support partial responses   74
Rule: The query component of a URI should be used to embed linked resources   76
Processing Hypermedia   78
JavaScript Clients   79
Rule: JSONP should be supported to provide multi-origin read access from JavaScript   80
Rule: CORS should be supported to provide multi-origin read/write access from JavaScript   82
Recap   83

7. **Final Thoughts** **85**
State of the Art   85
Uniform Implementation   86
Principle: REST API designs differ more than necessary   86
Principle: A REST API should be designed, not coded   87
Principle: Programmers and their organizations benefit from consistency   88
Principle: A REST API should be created using a GUI tool   89
Recap   91

Appendix: My First REST API **93**

Preface

Greetings Program!

Representational State Transfer (REST) is a technical description of how the World Wide Web* works. Specifically, REST tells us how the Web achieves its great scale. If the Web can be said to have an "operating system," its architectural style is REST.

A REST Application Programming Interface (REST API) is a type of web server that enables a client, either user-operated or automated, to access *resources* that model a system's data and functions.

This book is a REST API designer's style guide and reference. It proposes a set of *rules* that you can leverage to design and develop REST APIs.

Conventions Used in This Book

The following typographical conventions are used in this book:

Italic
    Indicates new terms, URLs, email addresses, filenames, and file extensions.

`Constant width`
    Used for program listings, as well as within paragraphs to refer to program elements such as variable or function names, databases, data types, environment variables, statements, and keywords.

`Constant width bold`
    Shows commands or other text that should be typed literally by the user.

`Constant width italic`
    Shows text that should be replaced with user-supplied values or by values determined by context.

---

* The "World Wide Web" is more commonly known as "the Web," which is how this book refers to it.

This icon signifies a tip, suggestion, or general note.

 This icon indicates a warning or caution.

Using Code Examples

This book is here to help you get your job done. In general, you may use the code in this book in your programs and documentation. You do not need to contact us for permission unless you're reproducing a significant portion of the code. For example, writing a program that uses several chunks of code from this book does not require permission. Selling or distributing a CD-ROM of examples from O'Reilly books does require permission. Answering a question by citing this book and quoting example code does not require permission. Incorporating a significant amount of example code from this book into your product's documentation does require permission.

We appreciate, but do not require, attribution. An attribution usually includes the title, author, publisher, and ISBN. For example: "*REST API Design Rulebook* by Mark Massé (O'Reilly). Copyright 2012 Mark Massé, 978-1-449-31050-9."

If you feel your use of code examples falls outside fair use or the permission given above, feel free to contact us at *permissions@oreilly.com*.

Safari® Books Online

 Safari Books Online is an on-demand digital library that lets you easily search over 7,500 technology and creative reference books and videos to find the answers you need quickly.

With a subscription, you can read any page and watch any video from our library online. Read books on your cell phone and mobile devices. Access new titles before they are available for print, and get exclusive access to manuscripts in development and post feedback for the authors. Copy and paste code samples, organize your favorites, download chapters, bookmark key sections, create notes, print out pages, and benefit from tons of other time-saving features.

O'Reilly Media has uploaded this book to the Safari Books Online service. To have full digital access to this book and others on similar topics from O'Reilly and other publishers, sign up for free at *http://my.safaribooksonline.com*.

How to Contact Us

Please address comments and questions concerning this book to the publisher:

O'Reilly Media, Inc.
1005 Gravenstein Highway North
Sebastopol, CA 95472
800-998-9938 (in the United States or Canada)
707-829-0515 (international or local)
707-829-0104 (fax)

We have a web page for this book, where we list errata, examples, and any additional information. You can access this page at:

http://oreilly.com/catalog/0636920021575

To comment or ask technical questions about this book, send email to:

bookquestions@oreilly.com

For more information about our books, courses, conferences, and news, see our website at *http://www.oreilly.com*.

Find us on Facebook: *http://facebook.com/oreilly*

Follow us on Twitter: *http://twitter.com/oreillymedia*

Watch us on YouTube: *http://www.youtube.com/oreillymedia*

Acknowledgments

I could not have written this book without the help of the folks mentioned here.

Tim Berners-Lee

As a member of the World Wide Web generation, I have spent my entire career as a software engineer working in, and adding to, the Web. I am eternally grateful to Tim Berners-Lee for his "WorldWideWeb" project. A triumph; huge success.

Roy Fielding

Roy Fielding's pioneering Ph.D. dissertation was the primary inspiration for this book. If you want to learn all about REST from its original author, I highly recommend that you read Fielding's dissertation.[†]

[†] Fielding, Roy Thomas. *Architectural Styles and the Design of Network-based Software Architectures*, Doctoral dissertation, University of California, Irvine, 2000 (*http://www.ics.uci.edu/~fielding/pubs/dissertation/top.htm*).

Leonard Richardson

In an effort to distinguish between *RESTful* and other Web API designs, Leonard Richardson proposed‡ what has come to be known as the "Richardson Maturity Model." In his model, Richardson outlined three distinct levels of REST API maturity:

1. URI
2. HTTP
3. Hypermedia

Each level corresponds with an aspect of the Web's *uniform interface* that an API must embrace in order to be considered RESTful. The maturity model's level-based classification system has helped me evaluate and concisely communicate the RESTfulness of many Web API designs.§

O'Reilly Media, Inc.

I have been a fan of O'Reilly's books for as long as I've been programming. Working on this project with O'Reilly's Simon St. Laurent has been an incredible experience and an honest to goodness dream come true for me. I am greatly honored to have been given this opportunity and I thank Simon and everyone at O'Reilly Media for their support and encouragement.

Additionally, this book would not exist without these foundational books, also published by O'Reilly:

- Richardson, Leonard, and Sam Ruby. *RESTful Web Services*. Sebastopol: O'Reilly Media, Inc., 2007.
- Allamaraju, Subbu. *RESTful Web Services Cookbook*. Sebastopol: O'Reilly Media, Inc., 2010.
- Webber, Jim, Savas Parastatidis, and Ian Robinson. *REST in Practice: Hypermedia and Systems Architecture*. Sebastopol: O'Reilly Media, Inc., 2010.

Technical Reviewers

I am indebted to this book's technical reviewers. Each one took the time to read through rough drafts of this book and provided insightful feedback that improved the end result. Many thanks to: Mike Amundsen, Ryan Christianson, Jason Guenther, Brian Jackson, Greg Katz, Will Merydith, Leonard Richardson, Daniel Roop, Nigel Simpson, and Cameron Stevens.

---

‡ *http://www.crummy.com/writing/speaking/2008-QCon/act3.html*

§ Leonard Richardson also co-authored the milestone book, *RESTful Web Services* (O'Reilly) which really helped move REST forward.

Colleagues

Will Wiess, Scott Thompson, Kelley Faraone, Eric Freeman, and Nick Choat supported my learning and teaching efforts over the past few years. Thank you all.

The REST Community

From a career perspective, this is an exciting time to be both working with and *using* the Web! This book was influenced by anyone who has ever posted a scrap of information about REST on the Web; or at least to those that search engines could find. Over the years, I have pored over too many "REST API" articles and examples to count. I know that each one helped shape my mental model of the best practices of REST API design.

Stuart Rackham

Thanks also to Stuart Rackham for *AsciiDoc*.‖ It is an awesome tool that made formatting this book a breeze.

Personal

My brother Mike Massé (*http://www.mikemasse.com*) is a Web-based rock star. His music provided the soundtrack for all my writing sessions. Mike's talents and passions have been a lifelong inspiration to me.

Thanks to my family (daughter, mom, dad, and sisters) for their patience and support while I was off the grid working on this book.

Finally, I thank Shawna Stine, for being the book's first reviewer and biggest fan.

‖ *http://www.methods.co.nz/asciidoc*

## CHAPTER 1

Introduction

Hello World Wide Web

The Web started in the "data acquisition and control" group at the European Organization for Nuclear Research (CERN), in Geneva, Switzerland. It began with a computer programmer who had a clever idea for a new software project.

In December of 1990, to facilitate the sharing of knowledge, Tim Berners-Lee started a non-profit software project that he called "WorldWideWeb."[*] After working diligently on his project for about a year, Berners-Lee had invented and implemented:

- The Uniform Resource Identifier (URI), a syntax that assigns each web document a unique address
- The HyperText Transfer Protocol[†] (HTTP), a message-based language that computers could use to communicate over the Internet.
- The HyperText Mark-up Language (HTML), to represent informative documents that contain links to related documents.
- The first web server.[‡]
- The first web browser, which Berners-Lee also named "WorldWideWeb" and later renamed "Nexus" to avoid confusion with the Web itself.
- The first WYSIWYG[§] HTML editor, which was built right into the browser.

---

[*] The WorldWideWeb project was later renamed the "World Wide Web," with added spaces.

[†] Berners-Lee, Tim. *The Original HTTP as defined in 1991*, W3C, 1991 (*http://www.w3.org/Protocols/HTTP/AsImplemented.html*).

[‡] The first web server is still up and running at *http://info.cern.ch*.

[§] WYSIWYG is an acronym for *What You See Is What You Get*.

On August 6, 1991, on the Web's first page, Berners-Lee wrote,

> The WorldWideWeb (W3) is a wide-area hypermedia information retrieval initiative aiming to give universal access to a large universe of documents.[||]

From that moment, the Web began to grow, at times exponentially. Within five years, the number of web users skyrocketed to 40 million. At one point, the number was doubling every two months. The "universe of documents" that Berners-Lee had described was indeed expanding.

In fact, the Web was growing too large, too fast, and it was heading toward collapse.

The Web's traffic was outgrowing the capacity of the Internet infrastructure. Additionally, the Web's core protocols were not uniformly implemented and they lacked support for caches and other stabilizing intermediaries. With such rapid expansion, it was unclear if the Web would scale to meet the increasing demand.

Web Architecture

In late 1993, Roy Fielding, co-founder of the Apache HTTP Server Project,[#] became concerned by the Web's scalability problem.

Upon analysis, Fielding recognized that the Web's scalability was governed by a set of key *constraints*. He and others set out to improve the Web's implementation with a pragmatic approach: uniformly satisfy all of the constraints so that the Web could continue to expand.

The constraints, which Fielding grouped into six categories and collectively referred to as the Web's *architectural style*, are:

1. Client-server
2. Uniform interface
3. Layered system
4. Cache
5. Stateless
6. Code-on-demand

Each constraint category is summarized in the following subsections.

[||] Berners-Lee, Tim. *World Wide Web*, W3C, 1991 (*http://www.w3.org/History/19921103-hypertext/ hypertext/WWW/TheProject.html*).

[#] *http://httpd.apache.org*.

Client–Server

The separation of concerns is the core theme of the Web's client-server constraints. The Web is a client-server based system, in which clients and servers have distinct parts to play. They may be implemented and deployed independently, using any language or technology, so long as they conform to the Web's *uniform interface*.

Uniform Interface

The interactions between the Web's components—meaning its clients, servers, and network-based intermediaries—depend on the uniformity of their interfaces. If any of the components stray from the established standards, then the Web's communication system breaks down.

Web components interoperate consistently within the uniform interface's four constraints, which Fielding identified as:

1. Identification of resources
2. Manipulation of resources through representations
3. Self-descriptive messages
4. Hypermedia as the engine of application state (HATEOAS)

The four interface constraints are summarized in the following subsections.

Identification of resources

Each distinct Web-based concept is known as a *resource* and may be addressed by a unique identifier, such as a URI. For example, a particular home page URI, like *http://www.oreilly.com*, uniquely identifies the concept of a specific website's root resource.

Manipulation of resources through representations

Clients manipulate representations of resources. The same exact resource can be represented to different clients in different ways. For example, a document might be represented as HTML to a web browser, and as JSON to an automated program. The key idea here is that the representation is a way to interact with the resource but it is not the resource itself. This conceptual distinction allows the resource to be represented in different ways and formats without ever changing its identifier.

Self-descriptive messages

A resource's *desired* state can be represented within a client's request message. A resource's *current* state may be represented within the response message that comes back from a server. As an example, a wiki page editor client may use a request message to transfer a representation that *suggests* a page update (new state) for a server-managed web page (resource). It is up to the server to accept or deny the client's request.

The self-descriptive messages may include *metadata* to convey additional details regarding the resource state, the representation format and size, and the message itself. An HTTP message provides *headers* to organize the various types of metadata into uniform fields.

Hypermedia as the engine of application state (HATEOAS)

A resource's state representation includes links to related resources. Links are the threads that weave the Web together by allowing users to traverse information and applications in a meaningful and directed manner. The presence, or absence, of a link on a page is an important part of the resource's current state.

Layered System

The layered system constraints enable network-based intermediaries such as proxies and gateways to be *transparently* deployed between a client and server using the Web's uniform interface. Generally speaking, a network-based intermediary will intercept client-server communication for a specific purpose. Network-based intermediaries are commonly used for enforcement of security, response caching, and load balancing.

Cache

Caching is one of web architecture's most important constraints. The cache constraints instruct a web server to declare the *cacheability* of each response's data. Caching response data can help to reduce client-perceived latency, increase the overall availability and reliability of an application, and control a web server's load. In a word, caching reduces the overall *cost* of the Web.

A cache may exist anywhere along the network path between the client and server. They can be in an organization's web server network, within specialized content delivery networks (CDNs), or inside a client itself.

Stateless

The stateless constraint dictates that a web server is not required to memorize the state of its client applications. As a result, each client must include all of the contextual information that it considers relevant in each interaction with the web server. Web servers ask clients to manage the complexity of communicating their application state so that the web server can service a much larger number of clients. This trade-off is a key contributor to the scalability of the Web's architectural style.

Code-On-Demand

The Web makes heavy use of code-on-demand, a constraint which enables web servers to temporarily transfer executable programs, such as scripts or plug-ins, to clients.

Code-on-demand tends to establish a technology coupling between web servers and their clients, since the client must be able to understand and execute the code that it downloads on-demand from the server. For this reason, code-on-demand is the only constraint of the Web's architectural style that is considered optional. Web browser-hosted technologies like Java applets, JavaScript, and Flash exemplify the code-on-demand constraint.

Web Standards

Fielding worked alongside Tim Berners-Lee and others to increase the Web's scalability. To *standardize* their designs, they wrote a specification for the new version of the Hypertext Transfer Protocol, HTTP/1.1.[*] They also formalized the syntax of Uniform Resource Identifiers (URI) in RFC 3986.[†]

Adoption of these standards quickly spread across the Web and paved the way for its continued growth.

REST

In the year 2000, after the Web's scalability crisis was averted, Fielding named and described the Web's architectural style in his Ph.D. dissertation.[‡] "Representational State Transfer" (REST) is the name that Fielding gave to his description[§] of the Web's architectural style, which is composed of the constraints outlined above.

REST APIs

Web services are purpose-built web servers that support the needs of a site or any other application. Client programs use application programming interfaces (APIs) to communicate with web services. Generally speaking, an API exposes a set of data and functions to facilitate interactions between computer programs and allow them to exchange information. As depicted in Figure 1-1, a Web API is the *face* of a web service, directly listening and responding to client requests.

The REST architectural style is commonly applied to the design of APIs for modern web services. A Web API conforming to the REST architectural style is a *REST API*.

---

[*] Fielding, Roy T., Tim Berners-Lee, et al. *HTTP/1.1*, RFC 2616, RFC Editor, 1999 (*http://www.rfc-editor.org/ rfc/rfc2616.txt*).

[†] Berners-Lee, Tim, Roy T. Fielding, et al. *Uniform Resource Identifier (URI): Generic Syntax*, RFC 3986, RFC Editor, 2005 (*http://www.rfc-editor.org/rfc/rfc3986.txt*).

[‡] Fielding, Roy Thomas. *Architectural Styles and the Design of Network-based Software Architectures*, Doctoral dissertation, University of California, Irvine, 2000 (*http://www.ics.uci.edu/~fielding/pubs/dissertation/top .htm*).

[§] "REST" is the name of the description, or derivation, of the Web's architectural style.

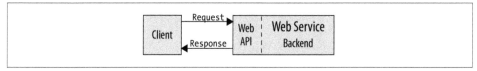

Figure 1-1. Web API

Having a REST API makes a web service "RESTful." A REST API consists of an assembly of interlinked resources. This set of resources is known as the REST API's *resource model*.

Well-designed REST APIs can attract client developers to use web services. In today's open market where rival web services are competing for attention, an aesthetically pleasing REST API design is a must-have feature.

REST API Design

For many of us, designing a REST API can sometimes feel more like an art than a science. Some best practices for REST API design are implicit in the HTTP standard, while other pseudo-standard approaches have emerged over the past few years. Yet today, we must continue to seek out answers to a slew of questions, such as:

- When should URI path segments be named with plural nouns?
- Which request method should be used to update resource state?
- How do I map *non-CRUD* operations to my URIs?
- What is the appropriate HTTP response status code for a given scenario?
- How can I manage the versions of a resource's state representations?
- How should I structure a hyperlink in JSON?

Rules

This book presents a set of REST API design *rules* that aim to provide clear and concise answers to the nagging questions listed above. The rules are here to help you design REST APIs with consistency that can be leveraged by the clients that use them. These rules can be followed as a complete set or *a la carte*. You may contest the rules, but I believe that each one warrants careful consideration.

Many of this book's design rules are drawn from the best practices that have become *de facto* standards. If you have some experience with the design of REST APIs, then you are likely to be familiar with the rules related to URI design in Chapter 2 and the use of HTTP in Chapter 3. In contrast, most of the rules presented in Chapter 4 and Chapter 5 (particularly those that deal with media types and representational forms) are my solutions in the absence of consensus.

When used in the context of rules, the *key words*: "must," "must not," "required," "shall," "shall not," "should," "should not," "recommended," "may," and "optional" are to be interpreted as described in RFC 2119.‖

WRML

I've invented a conceptual framework called the Web Resource Modeling Language (WRML) to assist with the design and implementation of REST APIs. WRML, pronounced like "wormle," originated as a resource model diagramming technique that uses a set of basic shapes to represent each of the resource archetypes discussed in "Resource Archetypes" on page 15. The scope of WRML increased with the creation of the *application/wrml* media type,# which has pluggable *format* and *schema* components, as described in "Media Type Design" on page 41. In many of the book's later rules, I'll use ideas from WRML to fill in the gaps in current best practices with rational advice for common situations.

In Chapters 5 and 6 you'll notice that many of the rules include examples that use the JavaScript Object Notation (JSON) to format representations.* JSON is an important format that has many advantages, such as native JavaScript support, near-ubiquitous adoption, and familiar syntax. However, by itself the JSON format does not provide uniform structures for some of the most important REST API concepts, specifically links, link relations, and schemas. The rules in "Hypermedia Representation" on page 49 and "Schema Representation" on page 59, use WRML to demonstrate JSON-formatted representational forms for each of these core constructs.

Finally, Chapter 7 asserts that uniformity of API design is not merely an *academic* pursuit. On the contrary it holds the promise of improving the lives of programmers by empowering us with a rich set of development tools and frameworks that we can leverage to design and develop REST APIs.

Recap

This chapter presented a synopsis of the Web's invention and stabilization. It motivated the book's rule-oriented presentation and introduced WRML, a conceptual framework whose ideas promote a uniform REST API design methodology. Subsequent chapters will build on this foundation to help us leverage REST in API designs. Table 1-1 summarizes the vocabulary terms that were introduced in this chapter.

‖ Bradner, Scott. *Key words for use in RFCs to Indicate Requirement Levels*, RFC 2119, RFC Editor, 1997 (*http://www.rfc-editor.org/rfc/rfc2119.txt*).

The *application/wrml* media type's IANA registration is pending—see *http://www.wrml.org* for the most up-to-date information.

* *http://www.json.org*

Table 1-1. Vocabulary review

Term	Description
Application Programming Interface (API)	Exposes a set of data and functions to facilitate interactions between computer programs.
Architectural constraint	Limits the behavior of a system's components to enforce uniformity and achieve some desired property.
Architectural style	In his Ph.D. dissertation, Roy Fielding used this term to describe a set of constraints that restrict the behavior of a system's interconnected components.
Cache	REST constraints that enable network-based intermediaries to hold on to resource state representations, which helps web servers meet the demands of their clients.
Client—server	REST constraints that separate the concerns of its two primary components, which allows their implementations to evolve independently.
Code-on-demand	A REST constraint that optionally allows a web server to transfer executable programs to its clients on an as-needed basis.
Entity body	Section of an HTTP message that is designated to hold the (optional) content, which may be a resource representation.
Entity headers	Section of an HTTP message that can communicate meta information regarding a resource and its representation.
HATEOAS	Acronym that stands for REST's "Hypermedia as the Engine of Application State" uniform interface constraint, which refers to the practice of providing a state-aware list of links to convey a resource's available "actions."
Hypermedia	An extension of hypertext that enables multiple formats to be combined and tethered together with links to design a multi-media information network.
Hypertext	Text-based documents containing embedded links to related documents, which creates a navigable mesh of information.
HyperText Mark-up Language (HTML)	Created by Tim Berners-Lee to represent the state of a web resource's information and relationships.
HyperText Transfer Protocol (HTTP)	Originally developed by Tim Berners-Lee, this is a message-based language that computers could use to communicate over the Internet.
Hypertext Transfer Protocol version 1.1 (HTTP/1.1)	Roy Fielding, Tim Berners-Lee, and others contributed to the standardization of this most recent version of the communication protocol.
JavaScript	A powerful scripting language that is commonly used by web developers.
JavaScript Object Notation (JSON)	A standardized text format that was derived from JavaScript and is used for structured data exchange.
Layered system	REST constraints that enable network-based intermediaries to sit between a client and server without compromising the uniform interface constraints.
Media type	A syntax that describes the form of content.
Message	Self-descriptive envelope that is often used to carry a representation of a resource's state.
Representation	The formatted state of a resource, which may be transferred via messages that are passed between components.

Term	Description
Representational State Transfer (REST)	Roy Fielding's derivation of the Web's architectural style.
Request message	Sent from clients to interact with a URI-indicated web resource. May contain a representation that suggests a resource state.
Resource	Any Web-based concept that can be referenced by a unique identifier and manipulated via the uniform interface.
Resource identifier	A universally unique ID of a specific Web-based concept.
Resource model	An assembly of interlinked Web-based concepts.
Resource state representation	The rendered state of a web server-owned resource; transferred between an application's client and server.
Response message	Returned from servers to indicate the results of a client's request. May contain a representation to convey a resource state.
REST API	A web service interface that conforms to the Web's architectural style.
Scalability	The ability to gracefully handle an increasing workload.
Stateless	A REST constraint that restricts a web server from holding on to any client-specific state information, which helps it support more clients.
Uniform interface	A set of four REST constraints that standardize the communication between Web-based components.
Uniform Resource Identifier (URI)	A syntax invented by Tim Berners-Lee to assign each web resource a unique ID.
Web API	Used by clients to interact with a web service.
Web browser (browser)	Common type of web client. Tim Berners-Lee developed the first one, which was able to view and edit HTML documents.
Web client (client)	A computer program that follows REST's uniform interface in order to accept and transfer resource state representations to servers.
Web component (component)	A client, network-based intermediary, or server that complies with REST's uniform interface.
Web Resource Modeling Language (WRML)	A conceptual framework whose ideas can be leveraged to design and implement uniform REST APIs.
Web server (server)	A computer program that follows REST's uniform interface constraints in order to accept and transfer resource state representations to clients.
Web service	A web server programmed with specific, often reusable, logic.

## CHAPTER 2

Identifier Design with URIs

URIs

REST APIs use Uniform Resource Identifiers (URIs) to address resources. On today's Web, URI designs range from *masterpieces* that clearly communicate the API's resource model like:

```
http://api.example.restapi.org/france/paris/louvre/leonardo-da-vinci/mona-lisa
```

to those that are much harder for *people* to understand, such as:

```
http://api.example.restapi.org/68dd0-a9d3-11e0-9f1c-0800200c9a66
```

Tim Berners-Lee included a note about the opacity of URIs in his "Axioms of Web Architecture" list:

> The only thing you can use an identifier for is to refer to an object. When you are not dereferencing, you should not look at the contents of the URI string to gain other information.
>
> —Tim Berners-Lee *http://www.w3.org/DesignIssues/Axioms.html*

As discussed in Chapter 5, clients must follow the linking paradigm of the Web and treat URIs as opaque identifiers. That said, REST API designers should create URIs that convey a REST API's resource model to its potential client developers.

This chapter introduces a set of design rules for REST API URIs.

URI Format

The rules presented in this section pertain to the *format* of a URI. RFC 3986[*] defines the generic URI syntax as shown below:

```
URI = scheme "://" authority "/" path [ "?" query ] [ "#" fragment ]
```

---

[*] Berners-Lee, Tim, Roy T. Fielding, et al. *Uniform Resource Identifier (URI): Generic Syntax*, RFC 3986, RFC Editor, 1998 (*http://www.rfc-editor.org/rfc/rfc3986.txt*).

Rule: Forward slash separator (/) must be used to indicate a hierarchical relationship

The forward slash (/) character is used in the path portion of the URI to indicate a hierarchical relationship between resources. For example:

```
http://api.canvas.restapi.org/shapes/polygons/quadrilaterals/squares
```

Rule: A trailing forward slash (/) should not be included in URIs

As the last character within a URI's path, a forward slash (/) adds no semantic value and may cause confusion. REST APIs should not expect a trailing slash and should not include them in the links that they provide to clients.

Many web components and frameworks will treat the following two URIs equally:

```
http://api.canvas.restapi.org/shapes/
http://api.canvas.restapi.org/shapes
```

However, every character within a URI *counts* toward a resource's unique identity. Two different URIs map to two different resources. If the URIs differ, then so do the resources, and vice versa. Therefore, a REST API must generate and communicate clean URIs and should be intolerant of any client's attempts to identify a resource imprecisely. More forgiving APIs may redirect clients to URIs without a trailing forward slash (as described in "Rule: 301 ("Moved Permanently") should be used to relocate resources" on page 29).

Rule: Hyphens (-) should be used to improve the readability of URIs

To make your URIs easy for people to scan and interpret, use the hyphen (-) character to improve the readability of names in long path segments. Anywhere you would use a space or hyphen in English, you should use a hyphen in a URI. For example:

```
http://api.example.restapi.org/blogs/mark-masse/entries/this-is-my-first-post
```

Rule: Underscores (_) should not be used in URIs

Text viewer applications (browsers, editors, etc.) often underline URIs to provide a visual cue that they are *clickable*. Depending on the application's font, the underscore (_) character can either get partially obscured or completely hidden by this underlining. To avoid this confusion, use hyphens (-) instead of underscores (as described in "Rule: Hyphens (-) should be used to improve the readability of URIs" on page 12).

Rule: Lowercase letters should be preferred in URI paths

When convenient, lowercase letters are preferred in URI paths since capital letters can sometimes cause problems. RFC 3986 defines URIs as case-sensitive except for the scheme and host components. For example:

```
http://api.example.restapi.org/my-folder/my-doc  ❶
HTTP://API.EXAMPLE.RESTAPI.ORG/my-folder/my-doc  ❷
http://api.example.restapi.org/My-Folder/my-doc  ❸
```

❶ This URI is fine.

❷ The URI format specification (RFC 3986) considers this URI to be identical to URI #1.

❸ This URI is *not* the same as URIs 1 and 2, which may cause unnecessary confusion.

Rule: File extensions should not be included in URIs

On the Web, the period (.) character is commonly used to separate the file name and extension portions of a URI. A REST API should not include *artificial* file extensions in URIs to indicate the format of a message's entity body. Instead, they should rely on the media type, as communicated through the Content-Type header, to determine how to process the body's content. For more about media types, see the section "Media Types" on page 39.

```
http://api.college.restapi.org/students/3248234/transcripts/2005/fall.json  ❶
http://api.college.restapi.org/students/3248234/transcripts/2005/fall       ❷
```

❶ File extensions should *not* be used to indicate format preference.

❷ REST API clients should be encouraged to utilize HTTP's provided format selection mechanism, the Accept request header, as discussed in the section "Rule: Media type negotiation should be supported when multiple representations are available" on page 43.

 To enable simple links and easy debugging, a REST API may support media type selection via a query parameter as discussed in the section "Rule: Media type selection using a query parameter may be supported" on page 44.

URI Authority Design

This section covers the naming conventions that should be used for the authority portion of a REST API.

Rule: Consistent subdomain names should be used for your APIs

The top-level domain and first subdomain names (e.g., soccer.restapi.org) of an API should identify its service owner. The full domain name of an API should add a subdomain named `api`. For example:

```
http://api.soccer.restapi.org
```

Rule: Consistent subdomain names should be used for your client developer portal

Many REST APIs have an associated website, known as a *developer portal*, to help on-board new clients with documentation, forums, and self-service provisioning of secure API access keys. If an API provides a developer portal, by convention it should have a subdomain labeled `developer`. For example:

```
http://developer.soccer.restapi.org
```

Resource Modeling

The URI path conveys a REST API's resource model, with each forward slash separated path segment corresponding to a unique resource within the model's hierarchy. For example, this URI design:

```
http://api.soccer.restapi.org/leagues/seattle/teams/trebuchet
```

indicates that each of these URIs should also identify an addressable resource:

```
http://api.soccer.restapi.org/leagues/seattle/teams
http://api.soccer.restapi.org/leagues/seattle
http://api.soccer.restapi.org/leagues
http://api.soccer.restapi.org
```

Resource modeling is an exercise that establishes your API's key concepts. This process is similar to the data modeling for a relational database schema or the classical modeling of an object-oriented system.

Before diving directly into the design of URI paths, it may be helpful to first think about the REST API's resource model.

Resource Archetypes

When modeling an API's resources, we can start with the some basic resource *arche-types*. Like design patterns, the resource archetypes help us consistently communicate the structures and behaviors that are commonly found in REST API designs. A REST API is composed of four distinct resource archetypes: *document*, *collection*, *store*, and *controller*.

 In order to communicate a clear and clean resource model to its clients, a REST API should align each resource with only one of these archetypes. For uniformity's sake, resist the temptation to design resources that are *hybrids* of more than one archetype. Instead, consider designing separate resources that are related hierarchically and/or through links, as discussed in Chapter 5.

Each of these resource archetypes is described in the subsections that follow.

Document

A document resource is a singular concept that is akin to an object instance or database record. A document's state representation typically includes both *fields* with values and *links* to other related resources. With its fundamental field and link-based structure, the document type is the conceptual *base archetype* of the other resource archetypes. In other words, the three other resource archetypes can be viewed as specializations of the document archetype.

Each URI below identifies a document resource:

```
http://api.soccer.restapi.org/leagues/seattle
http://api.soccer.restapi.org/leagues/seattle/teams/trebuchet
http://api.soccer.restapi.org/leagues/seattle/teams/trebuchet/players/mike
```

A document may have child resources that represent its specific subordinate concepts. With its ability to bring many different resource types together under a single parent, a document is a logical candidate for a REST API's root resource, which is also known as the *docroot*. The example URI below identifies the docroot, which is the Soccer REST API's advertised entry point:

```
http://api.soccer.restapi.org
```

Collection

A collection resource is a server-managed *directory* of resources. Clients may propose new resources to be added to a collection. However, it is up to the collection to choose to create a new resource, or not. A collection resource chooses what it wants to contain and also decides the URIs of each contained resource.

Each URI below identifies a collection resource:

```
http://api.soccer.restapi.org/leagues
http://api.soccer.restapi.org/leagues/seattle/teams
http://api.soccer.restapi.org/leagues/seattle/teams/trebuchet/players
```

Store

A store is a client-managed resource repository. A store resource lets an API client put resources in, get them back out, and decide when to delete them. On their own, stores do not create new resources; therefore a store never generates new URIs. Instead, each stored resource has a URI that was chosen by a client when it was initially put into the store.

The example interaction below shows a user (with ID *1234*) of a client program using a fictional Soccer REST API to insert a document resource named *alonso* in his or her store of *favorites*:

```
PUT /users/1234/favorites/alonso
```

Controller

A controller resource models a procedural concept. Controller resources are like executable functions, with parameters and return values; inputs and outputs.

Like a traditional web application's use of HTML forms, a REST API relies on controller resources to perform application-specific actions that cannot be logically mapped to one of the standard methods (create, retrieve, update, and delete, also known as CRUD).

Controller names typically appear as the last segment in a URI path, with no *child* resources to follow them in the hierarchy. The example below shows a controller resource that allows a client to resend an alert to a user:

```
POST /alerts/245743/resend
```

URI Path Design

Each URI path segment, separated by forward slashes (/), represents a design opportunity. Assigning meaningful values to each path segment helps to clearly communicate the hierarchical structure of a REST API's resource model design.

Figure 2-1 uses WRML notation† to exemplify the correlation of a URI path's design with the resource model that it conveys.

---

† Web Resource Modeling Language (WRML) was introduced in "WRML" on page 7

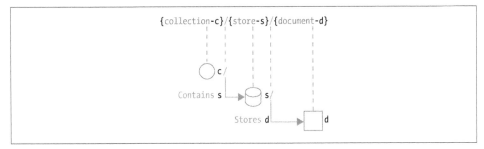

Figure 2-1. WRML diagram of a URI's associated resource model

This section provides rules relating to the design of meaningful URI paths.

Rule: A singular noun should be used for document names

A URI representing a document resource should be named with a singular noun or noun phrase path segment.

For example, the URI for a single player document would have the singular form:

```
http://api.soccer.restapi.org/leagues/seattle/teams/trebuchet/players/claudio
```

Rule: A plural noun should be used for collection names

A URI identifying a collection should be named with a plural noun, or noun phrase, path segment. A collection's name should be chosen to reflect what it uniformly contains.

For example, the URI for a collection of player documents uses the plural noun form of its contained resources:

```
http://api.soccer.restapi.org/leagues/seattle/teams/trebuchet/players
```

Rule: A plural noun should be used for store names

A URI identifying a store of resources should be named with a plural noun, or noun phrase, as its path segment. The URI for a store of music playlists may use the plural noun form as follows:

```
http://api.music.restapi.org/artists/mikemassedotcom/playlists
```

Rule: A verb or verb phrase should be used for controller names

Like a computer program's function, a URI identifying a controller resource should be named to indicate its action. For example:

```
http://api.college.restapi.org/students/morgan/register
http://api.example.restapi.org/lists/4324/dedupe
```

```
http://api.ognom.restapi.org/dbs/reindex
http://api.build.restapi.org/qa/nightly/runTestSuite
```

Rule: Variable path segments may be substituted with identity-based values

Some URI path segments are *static*; meaning they have fixed names that may be chosen by the REST API's designer. Other URI path segments are *variable*, which means that they are automatically filled in with some identifier that may help provide the URI with its uniqueness. The *URI Template* syntax‡ allows designers to clearly name both the static and variable segments. A URI template includes variables that must be substituted before resolution. The URI template example below has three variables (*leagueId*, *teamId*, and *playerId*):

```
http://api.soccer.restapi.org/leagues/{leagueId}/teams/{teamId}/players/{playerId}
```

The substitution of a URI template's variables may be done by a REST API or its clients. Each substitution may use a numeric or alphanumeric identifier, as shown in the examples below:

```
http://api.soccer.restapi.org/leagues/seattle/teams/trebuchet/players/21  ❶
http://api.soccer.restapi.org/games/3fd65a60-cb8b-11e0-9572-0800200c9a66  ❷
```

❶ Conceptually, the value 21 occupies a variable path segment slot named *playerId*.

❷ The UUID value fills in the *gameId* variable.

 A REST API's clients must consider URIs to be the *only* meaningful resource identifiers. Although other backend system identifiers (such as database IDs) may appear in a URI's path, they are meaningless to client code. By establishing URIs as the only IDs, a REST API's backend implementation may evolve over time without impacting its existing clients.

Rule: CRUD function names should not be used in URIs

URIs should not be used to indicate that a CRUD§ function is performed. URIs should be used to uniquely identify resources, and they should be named as described in the rules above. As discussed in "Request Methods" on page 23, HTTP request methods should be used to indicate which CRUD function is performed.

For example, this API interaction design is preferred:

```
DELETE /users/1234
```

---

‡ *http://tools.ietf.org/html/draft-gregorio-uritemplate*.

§ CRUD is an acronym that stands for create, read, update, delete—the four standard, storage-oriented functions.

The following anti-patterns exemplify what *not* to do:

```
GET /deleteUser?id=1234
GET /deleteUser/1234
DELETE /deleteUser/1234
POST /users/1234/delete
```

URI Query Design

This section provides rules relating to the design of URI queries. Recall from RFC 3986 that a URI's optional query comes after the path and before the optional fragment:

```
URI = scheme "://" authority "/" path [ "?" query ] [ "#" fragment ]
```

As a component of a URI, the query contributes to the unique identification of a resource. Consider the following example:

```
http://api.college.restapi.org/students/morgan/send-sms  ❶
http://api.college.restapi.org/students/morgan/send-sms?text=hello  ❷
```

❶ The URI of a controller resource that sends an sms message.

❷ The URI of a controller resource that sends an sms message with a text value of hello.

The query component of a URI contains a set of parameters to be interpreted as a variation or derivative of the resource that is hierarchically identified by the path component. So, while these two resources are not the same, they are very closely related.

The query component can provide clients with additional interaction capabilities such as ad hoc searching and filtering. Therefore, unlike the other elements of a URI, the query part may be transparent to a REST API's client.

The *entirety* of a resource's URI should be treated opaquely by basic network-based intermediaries such as HTTP caches. Caches must not vary their behavior based on the presence or absence of a query in a given URI. Specifically, response messages must not be excluded from caches based solely upon the presence of a query in the requested URI. As discussed later in Chapter 4, HTTP headers, *not* queries, must be used to direct a cache intermediary's behavior.

Rule: The query component of a URI may be used to filter collections or stores

A URI's query component is a natural fit for supplying search criteria to a collection or store. Let's take a look at an example:

```
GET /users  ❶
GET /users?role=admin  ❷
```

❶ The response message's state representation contains a listing of all the users in the collection.

❷ The response message's state representation contains a filtered list of all the users in the collection with a "role" value of admin.

Rule: The query component of a URI should be used to paginate collection or store results

A REST API client should use the query component to paginate collection and store results with the `pageSize` and `pageStartIndex` parameters. The `pageSize` parameter specifies the maximum number of contained elements to return in the response. The `pageStartIndex` parameter specifies the zero-based index of the first element to return in the response. For example:

```
GET /users?pageSize=25&pageStartIndex=50
```

When the complexity of a client's pagination (or filtering) requirements exceeds the simple formatting capabilities of the query part, consider designing a special controller resource that *partners* with a collection or store. For example, the following controller may accept more complex inputs via a request's entity body instead of the URI's query part:

```
POST /users/search
```

This design allows for custom range types and special sort orders to be easily specified in the client request message body. However, as detailed in Chapter 4, care must be taken to ensure that the controller's cacheable results are marked accordingly.

Recap

This chapter offered a set of design rules for REST API URIs. Table 2-1 summarizes the terms that were used in this chapter.

Table 2-1. Vocabulary review

Term	Description
Authority	A URI component that identifies the party with jurisdiction over the namespace defined by the remainder of the URI.
Collection	A resource archetype used to model a server-managed *directory* of resources.
Controller	A resource archetype used to model a procedural concept.
CRUD	An acronym that stands for the four classic storage-oriented functions: create, retrieve, update, and delete.
Developer portal	A Web-based graphical user interface that helps a REST API acquire new clients.
Docroot	A resource that is the hierarchical ancestor of all other resources within a REST API's model. This resource's URI should be the REST API's advertised entry point.
Document	A resource archetype used to model a singular concept.
Forward slash separator (/)	Used within the URI path component to separate hierarchically related resources.
Opacity of URIs	An axiom, originally described by Tim Berners-Lee, that governs the visibility of a resource identifier's composition.

Term	Description
Parent resource	The document, collection, or store that governs a given subordinate concept by preceding it within a URI's hierarchical path.
Query	A URI component that comes after the path and before the optional fragment.
Resource archetypes	A set of four intrinsic concepts (document, collection, store, and controller) that may be used to help describe a REST API's model.
Store	A resource archetype used to model a client-managed resource repository.
URI path segment	Part of a resource identifier that represents a single node within a larger, hierarchical resource model.
URI template	A resource identifier syntax that includes variables that must be substituted before resolution.

## CHAPTER 3

Interaction Design with HTTP

HTTP/1.1

REST APIs embrace all aspects of the HyperText Transfer Protocol, version 1.1[*] (HTTP/1.1) including its request methods, response codes, and message headers.

This book divides its coverage of HTTP between two chapters, with this chapter discussing request methods and response status codes. Incorporating metadata in a REST API design, with HTTP's request and response headers, is the subject of Chapter 4.

 A few of this chapter's examples use *curl (http://curl.haxx.se)*, the command-line, open-source web client that is available for most modern development platforms. For some common REST API-related development tasks, curl has some advantages over the browser. Specifically, curl allows easy access to HTTP's full feature set and it is *scriptable*, meaning that programmers can write simple shell scripts or batch files containing curl commands to test or use a REST API.

Request Methods

Clients specify the desired interaction method in the `Request-Line` part of an HTTP request message. RFC 2616 defines the `Request-Line` syntax as shown below:

```
Request-Line   = Method SP Request-URI SP HTTP-Version CRLF
```

Each HTTP method has specific, well-defined semantics within the context of a REST API's resource model. The purpose of `GET` is to retrieve a representation of a resource's state. `HEAD` is used to retrieve the metadata associated with the resource's state. `PUT` should be used to add a new resource to a store or update a resource. `DELETE` removes

---

[*] Fielding, Roy T., Tim Berners-Lee, et al. *HTTP/1.1*, RFC 2616, RFC Editor, 1999 (*http://www.rfc-editor.org/rfc/rfc2616.txt*).

a resource from its parent. POST should be used to create a new resource within a collection and execute controllers.

Rule: GET and POST must not be used to tunnel other request methods

Tunneling refers to any abuse of HTTP that masks or misrepresents a message's intent and undermines the protocol's transparency. A REST API must not compromise its design by misusing HTTP's request methods in an effort to accommodate clients with limited HTTP vocabulary. Always make proper use of the HTTP methods as specified by the rules in this section.

Rule: GET must be used to retrieve a representation of a resource

A REST API client uses the GET method in a request message to retrieve the state of a resource, in some representational form. A client's GET request message may contain headers but no body.

The architecture of the Web relies heavily on the nature of the GET method. Clients count on being able to repeat GET requests without causing side effects. Caches depend on the ability to serve cached representations without contacting the origin server.

In the example below, we can see how a client developer might use *curl* from a command shell to GET a representation of a "greeting" resource's current state:

```
$ curl -v http://api.example.restapi.org/greeting  ❶

> GET /greeting HTTP/1.1  ❷
> User-Agent: curl/7.20.1  ❸
> Host: api.example.restapi.org
> Accept: */*

< HTTP/1.1 200 OK  ❹
< Date: Sat, 20 Aug 2011 16:02:40 GMT  ❺
< Server: Apache
< Expires: Sat, 20 Aug 2011 16:03:40 GMT
< Cache-Control: max-age=60, must-revalidate
< ETag: text/html:hello world
< Content-Length: 130
< Last-Modified: Sat, 20 Aug 2011 16:02:17 GMT
< Vary: Accept-Encoding
< Content-Type: text/html

<!doctype html><head><meta charset="utf-8"><title>Greeting</title></head>  ❻
<body><div id="greeting">Hello World!</div></body></html>
```

❶ A command prompt showing the curl command. GET is curl's default method, so it doesn't need to be specified explicitly. The *-v* option makes the curl command's output more *verbose*.

❷ The request message's Request-Line indicates that the GET method was used on the greeting resource.

❸ The request message's list of headers starts here. HTTP's request and response headers are discussed in Chapter 4.

❹ The response message starts here, with the Status-Line discussed in "Response Status Codes" on page 28. The 200 OK status code tells curl that its request was successful.

❺ The response message's list of headers starts here.

❻ The response message's body starts here. In this example the body contains an HTML-formatted representation of a greeting message.

Rule: HEAD should be used to retrieve response headers

Clients use HEAD to retrieve the headers without a body. In other words, HEAD returns the same response as GET, except that the API returns an empty body. Clients can use this method to check whether a resource exists or to read its metadata.

The example below shows the curl command for retrieving headers with the HEAD method:

```
$ curl --head http://api.example.restapi.org/greeting

HTTP/1.1 200 OK  ❶
Date: Sat, 20 Aug 2011 16:02:40 GMT  ❷
Server: Apache
Expires: Sat, 20 Aug 2011 16:03:40 GMT
Cache-Control: max-age=60, must-revalidate
ETag: text/html:hello world
Content-Length: 130
Last-Modified: Sat, 20 Aug 2011 16:02:17 GMT
Vary: Accept-Encoding
Content-Type: text/html
```

❶ The response message starts here, with the Status-Line discussed in "Response Status Codes" on page 28. The 200 OK status code tells curl that its request was successful.

❷ The response message's list of headers starts here.

Like GET, a HEAD request message may contain headers but no body.

Rule: PUT must be used to both insert and update a stored resource

PUT must be used to add a new resource to a store, with a URI specified by the client. PUT must also be used to update or replace an already stored resource.

The example below demonstrates how a service-oriented REST API can provide a store resource that allows its client application's to persist their data as objects:

```
PUT /accounts/4ef2d5d0-cb7e-11e0-9572-0800200c9a66/buckets/objects/4321
```

The PUT request message must include a representation of a resource that the client wants to store. However, the body of the request may or may not be *exactly* the same as a client would receive from a subsequent GET request. For example, a REST API's store resource may allow clients to include only the mutable portions of the resource state in the request message's representation.

The section "Rule: Stores must support conditional PUT requests" on page 36 describes how a REST API should use HTTP headers to handle *overloading* the PUT method to both insert and update resources.

Rule: PUT must be used to update mutable resources

Clients must use the PUT request method to make changes to resources. The PUT request message may include a body that reflects the desired changes.

Rule: POST must be used to create a new resource in a collection

Clients use POST when attempting to create a new resource within a collection. The POST request's body contains the *suggested* state representation of the new resource to be added to the server-owned collection.

The example below demonstrates how a client uses POST to request a new addition to a collection:

```
POST /leagues/seattle/teams/trebuchet/players

# Note the request message may contain a representation that suggests the initial state
of the player to be created.
```

This is the first of two uses of the POST method within the context of REST API design. Metaphorically, this use of POST is analogous to "posting" a new message on a bulletin board.

Rule: POST must be used to execute controllers

Clients use the POST method to *invoke* the function-oriented controller resources. A POST request message may include both headers and a body as inputs to a controller resource's function.

HTTP designates POST as semantically open-ended. It allows the method to take any action, regardless of its repeatability or side effects. This makes POST the clear choice to be paired with the equally unrestricted controller resources.

Our REST API designs use POST, along with a targeted controller resource, to trigger all operations that cannot be intuitively mapped to one of the other core HTTP methods. In other words, the POST method should not be used to get, store, or delete resources —HTTP already provides specific methods for each of those functions.

HTTP calls the POST request method *unsafe* and *non-idempotent*, which means that its outcome is unpredictable and not guaranteed to be repeatable without potentially undesirable side effects. For example, a resubmitted web form that uses POST might run the risk of double billing a user's credit card. Controller resources trade a degree of transparency and robustness for the sake of flexibility.

The example below demonstrates how a controller can be executed using the POST request method:

```
POST /alerts/245743/resend
```

This is the second use of POST in the design of REST APIs. This use case resembles the fairly common concept of a runtime system's "PostMessage" mechanism, which allows functions to be invoked across some sort of boundary.

Rule: DELETE must be used to remove a resource from its parent

A client uses DELETE to request that a resource be completely removed from its parent, which is often a collection or store. Once a DELETE request has been processed for a given resource, the resource can no longer be found by clients. Therefore, any future attempt to retrieve the resource's state representation, using either GET or HEAD, must result in a 404 ("Not Found") status returned by the API.

The example below shows how a client might remove a document from a store:

```
DELETE /accounts/4ef2d5d0-cb7e-11e0-9572-0800200c9a66/buckets/objects/4321
```

The DELETE method has very specific semantics in HTTP, which must not be overloaded or stretched by a REST API's design. Specifically, an API should not distort the intended meaning of DELETE by mapping it to a lesser action that leaves the resource, and its URI, available to clients. For example, if an API wishes to provide a "soft" delete or some other state-changing interaction, it should employ a special controller resource and direct its clients to use POST instead of DELETE to interact.

Rule: OPTIONS should be used to retrieve metadata that describes a resource's available interactions

Clients may use the OPTIONS request method to retrieve resource metadata that includes an Allow header value. For example:

```
Allow: GET, PUT, DELETE
```

In response to an OPTIONS request, a REST API may include a body that includes further details about each interaction option. For example, the response body could contain a list of link relation forms, which are discussed in the section "Rule: A consistent form should be used to represent link relations" on page 52.

Response Status Codes

REST APIs use the Status-Line part of an HTTP response message to inform clients of their request's overarching result. RFC 2616 defines the Status-Line syntax as shown below:

```
Status-Line = HTTP-Version SP Status-Code SP Reason-Phrase CRLF
```

HTTP defines forty standard status codes that can be used to convey the results of a client's request. The status codes are divided into the five categories presented in Table 3-1.

Table 3-1. Response status code categories

Category	Description
1xx: Informational	Communicates transfer protocol-level information.
2xx: Success	Indicates that the client's request was accepted successfully.
3xx: Redirection	Indicates that the client must take some additional action in order to complete their request.
4xx: Client Error	This category of error status codes points the finger at clients.
5xx: Server Error	The server takes responsibility for these error status codes.

This section concisely describes how and when to use the subset of codes that apply to the design of a REST API.

Rule: 200 ("OK") should be used to indicate nonspecific success

In most cases, 200 is the code the client hopes to see. It indicates that the REST API successfully carried out whatever action the client requested, and that no more specific code in the 2xx series is appropriate. Unlike the 204 status code, a 200 response should include a response body.

Rule: 200 ("OK") must not be used to communicate errors in the response body

Always make proper use of the HTTP response status codes as specified by the rules in this section. In particular, a REST API must not be compromised in an effort to accommodate less sophisticated HTTP clients.

Rule: 201 ("Created") must be used to indicate successful resource creation

A REST API responds with the 201 status code whenever a collection creates, or a store adds, a new resource at the client's request. There may also be times when a new resource is created as a result of some controller action, in which case 201 would also be an appropriate response.

Rule: 202 ("Accepted") must be used to indicate successful start of an asynchronous action

A 202 response indicates that the client's request will be handled asynchronously. This response status code tells the client that the request appears valid, but it still may have problems once it's finally processed. A 202 response is typically used for actions that take a long while to process.

Controller resources may send 202 responses, but other resource types should not.

Rule: 204 ("No Content") should be used when the response body is intentionally empty

The 204 status code is usually sent out in response to a PUT, POST, or DELETE request, when the REST API declines to send back any status message or representation in the response message's body. An API may also send 204 in conjunction with a GET request to indicate that the requested resource exists, but has no state representation to include in the body.

Rule: 301 ("Moved Permanently") should be used to relocate resources

The 301 status code indicates that the REST API's resource model has been significantly redesigned and a new *permanent* URI has been assigned to the client's requested resource. The REST API should specify the new URI in the response's Location header.

Rule: 302 ("Found") should not be used

The intended semantics of the 302 response code have been misunderstood by programmers and incorrectly implemented in programs since version 1.0 of the HTTP protocol.† The confusion centers on whether it is appropriate for a client to always automatically issue a follow-up GET request to the URI in response's Location header, regardless of the original request's method. For the record, the intent of 302 is that this automatic redirect behavior only applies if the client's original request used either the GET or HEAD method.

To clear things up, HTTP 1.1 introduced status codes 303 ("See Other") and 307 ("Temporary Redirect"), either of which should be used instead of 302.

† In HTTP/1.0, the 302 status code's reason phrase was "Moved Temporarily."

Rule: 303 ("See Other") should be used to refer the client to a different URI

A 303 response indicates that a controller resource has finished its work, but instead of sending a potentially unwanted response body, it sends the client the URI of a response resource. This can be the URI of a temporary status message, or the URI to some already existing, more permanent, resource.

Generally speaking, the 303 status code allows a REST API to send a reference to a resource without forcing the client to download its state. Instead, the client may send a GET request to the value of the Location header.

Rule: 304 ("Not Modified") should be used to preserve bandwidth

This status code is similar to 204 ("No Content") in that the response body must be empty. The key distinction is that 204 is used when there is nothing to send in the body, whereas 304 is used when there *is* state information associated with a resource but the client already has the most recent version of the representation.

This status code is used in conjunction with conditional HTTP requests, discussed in Chapter 4.

Rule: 307 ("Temporary Redirect") should be used to tell clients to resubmit the request to another URI

HTTP/1.1 introduced the 307 status code to reiterate the originally intended semantics of the 302 ("Found") status code. A 307 response indicates that the REST API is not going to process the client's request. Instead, the client should resubmit the request to the URI specified by the response message's Location header.

A REST API can use this status code to assign a *temporary* URI to the client's requested resource. For example, a 307 response can be used to shift a client request over to another host.

Rule: 400 ("Bad Request") may be used to indicate nonspecific failure

400 is the generic client-side error status, used when no other 4xx error code is appropriate.

 For errors in the 4xx category, the response body may contain a document describing the client's error (unless the request method was HEAD). See "Error Representation" on page 68 for error response body design.

Rule: 401 ("Unauthorized") must be used when there is a problem with the client's credentials

A 401 error response indicates that the client tried to operate on a protected resource without providing the proper authorization. It may have provided the wrong credentials or none at all.

Rule: 403 ("Forbidden") should be used to forbid access regardless of authorization state

A 403 error response indicates that the client's request is formed correctly, but the REST API refuses to honor it. A 403 response is *not* a case of insufficient client credentials; that would be 401 ("Unauthorized").

REST APIs use 403 to enforce application-level permissions. For example, a client may be authorized to interact with some, but not all of a REST API's resources. If the client attempts a resource interaction that is outside of its permitted scope, the REST API should respond with 403.

Rule: 404 ("Not Found") must be used when a client's URI cannot be mapped to a resource

The 404 error status code indicates that the REST API can't map the client's URI to a resource.

Rule: 405 ("Method Not Allowed") must be used when the HTTP method is not supported

The API responds with a 405 error to indicate that the client tried to use an HTTP method that the resource does not allow. For instance, a read-only resource could support only GET and HEAD, while a controller resource might allow GET and POST, but not PUT or DELETE.

A 405 response must include the Allow header, which lists the HTTP methods that the resource supports. For example:

```
Allow: GET, POST
```

Rule: 406 ("Not Acceptable") must be used when the requested media type cannot be served

The 406 error response indicates that the API is not able to generate any of the client's preferred media types, as indicated by the Accept request header. For example, a client request for data formatted as *application/xml* will receive a 406 response if the API is only willing to format data as *application/json*.

Rule: 409 ("Conflict") should be used to indicate a violation of resource state

The 409 error response tells the client that they tried to put the REST API's resources into an impossible or inconsistent state. For example, a REST API may return this response code when a client tries to delete a non-empty store resource.

Rule: 412 ("Precondition Failed") should be used to support conditional operations

The 412 error response indicates that the client specified one or more preconditions in its request headers, effectively telling the REST API to carry out its request only if certain conditions were met. A 412 response indicates that those conditions were not met, so instead of carrying out the request, the API sends this status code.

See "Rule: Stores must support conditional PUT requests" on page 36 for an example use of the 412 status code.

Rule: 415 ("Unsupported Media Type") must be used when the media type of a request's payload cannot be processed

The 415 error response indicates that the API is not able to process the client's supplied media type, as indicated by the Content-Type request header. For example, a client request including data formatted as *application/xml* will receive a 415 response if the API is only willing to process data formatted as *application/json*.

Rule: 500 ("Internal Server Error") should be used to indicate API malfunction

500 is the generic REST API error response. Most web frameworks automatically respond with this response status code whenever they execute some request handler code that raises an exception.

A 500 error is never the client's fault and therefore it is reasonable for the client to retry the exact same request that triggered this response, and hope to get a different response.

Recap

This chapter presented the design principles for HTTP's request methods and response status codes. Table 3-2 summarizes the vocabulary terms that were introduced.

Table 3-2. Vocabulary review

Term	Description
DELETE	HTTP request method used to remove its parent.
GET	HTTP request method used to retrieve a representation of a resource's state.
HEAD	HTTP request method used to retrieve the metadata associated with the resource's state.
OPTIONS	HTTP request method used to retrieve metadata that describes a resource's available interactions.
POST	HTTP request method used to create a new resource within a collection or execute a controller.
PUT	HTTP request method used to insert a new resource into a store or update a mutable resource.
Request-Line	RFC 2616 defines its syntax as Method SP Request-URI SP HTTP-Version CRLF
Request method	Indicates the desired action to be performed on the request message's identified resource.
Response status code	A three-digit numeric value that is communicated by a server to indicate the result of a client's request.
Status-Line	RFC 2616 defines its syntax as: HTTP-Version SP Status-Code SP Reason-Phrase CRLF
Tunneling	An abuse of HTTP that masks or misrepresents a message's intent and undermines the protocol's transparency.

Table 3-3 recaps the standard usage HTTP's POST method for each of the four resource archetypes.

Table 3-3. POST request method summary

	Document	Collection	Store	Controller
POST	*error*	Create a new, contained resource	*error*	Execute the *function*

Table 3-4 summarizes the standard usage HTTP's other request methods for all resource types.

Table 3-4. HTTP request method summary

Method	Semantics
GET	Retrieve the complete state of a resource, in some representational form
HEAD	Retrieve the metadata state of a resource
PUT	Insert a new resource into a store or update an existing, mutable resource
DELETE	Remove the resource from its parent
OPTIONS	Retrieve metadata that describes a resource's available interactions

Tables 3-5 and 3-6 summarize the success and error status codes, respectively.

Table 3-5. HTTP response success code summary

Code	Name	Meaning
200	OK	Indicates a nonspecific success
201	Created	Sent primarily by collections and stores but sometimes also by controllers, to indicate that a new resource has been created
202	Accepted	Sent by controllers to indicate the start of an asynchronous action
204	No Content	Indicates that the body has been intentionally left blank
301	Moved Permanently	Indicates that a new *permanent* URI has been assigned to the client's requested resource
303	See Other	Sent by controllers to return results that it considers optional
304	Not Modified	Sent to preserve bandwidth (with conditional GET)
307	Temporary Redirect	Indicates that a *temporary* URI has been assigned to the client's requested resource

Table 3-6. HTTP response error code summary

Code	Name	Meaning
400	Bad Request	Indicates a nonspecific client error
401	Unauthorized	Sent when the client either provided invalid credentials or forgot to send them
402	Forbidden	Sent to deny access to a protected resource
404	Not Found	Sent when the client tried to interact with a URI that the REST API could not map to a resource
405	Method Not Allowed	Sent when the client tried to interact using an unsupported HTTP method
406	Not Acceptable	Sent when the client tried to request data in an unsupported media type format
409	Conflict	Indicates that the client attempted to violate resource state
412	Precondition Failed	Tells the client that one of its preconditions was not met
415	Unsupported Media Type	Sent when the client submitted data in an unsupported media type format
500	Internal Server Error	Tells the client that the API is having problems of its own

## CHAPTER 4

Metadata Design

HTTP Headers

Various forms of metadata may be conveyed through the *entity headers* contained within HTTP's request and response messages. HTTP defines a set of standard headers, some of which provide information about a requested resource. Other headers indicate something about the representation carried by the message. Finally, a few headers serve as directives to control intermediary caches.

This brief chapter suggests a set of rules to help REST API designers work with HTTP's standard headers.

Rule: Content-Type must be used

The `Content-Type` header names the *type* of data found within a request or response message's body. The value of this header is a specially formatted text string known as a *media type*, which is the subject of "Media Types" on page 39. Clients and servers rely on this header's value to tell them how to process the sequence of bytes in a message's body.

Rule: Content-Length should be used

The `Content-Length` header gives the size of the entity-body in bytes. In responses, this header is important for two reasons. First, a client can know whether it has read the correct number of bytes from the connection. Second, a client can make a `HEAD` request to find out how large the entity-body is, without downloading it.

Rule: Last-Modified should be used in responses

The `Last-Modified` header applies to response messages only. The value of this response header is a timestamp that indicates the last time that something happened to alter the representational state of the resource. Clients and cache intermediaries may rely on this header to determine the freshness of their local copies of a resource's state representation. This header should always be supplied in response to GET requests.

Rule: ETag should be used in responses

The value of ETag is an opaque string that identifies a specific "version" of the representational state contained in the response's *entity*. The entity is the HTTP message's payload, which is composed of a message's headers and body. The entity tag may be any string value, so long as it changes along with the resource's representation. This header should always be sent in response to GET requests.

Clients may choose to save an ETag header's value for use in future GET requests, as the value of the conditional If-None-Match request header. If the REST API concludes that the entity tag hasn't changed, then it can save time and bandwidth by not sending the representation again.

 Generating an ETag from a machine-specific value is a *bad idea*. Specifically don't generate ETag values from an inconsistent source, like a host-specific notion of a file's last modified time. It may result in different ETag values being attributed to the same representation, which is likely to confuse the API's clients and intermediaries.

Rule: Stores must support conditional PUT requests

A store resource uses the PUT method for both insert and update, which means it is difficult for a REST API to know the true *intent* of a client's PUT request. Through headers, HTTP provides the necessary support to help an API resolve any potential ambiguity. A REST API must rely on the client to include the If-Unmodified-Since and/ or If-Match request headers to express their intent. The If-Unmodified-Since request header asks the API to proceed with the operation if, and only if, the resource's state representation hasn't changed since the time indicated by the header's supplied timestamp value. The If-Match header's value is an entity tag, which the client remembers from an earlier response's ETag header value. The If-Match header makes the request conditional, based upon an exact match of the header's supplied entity tag value and the representational state's current entity tag value, as stored or computed by the REST API.

The following example illustrates how a REST API can support *conditional* PUT requests using these two headers.

Two client programs, client#1 and client#2, use a REST API's */objects* store resource to share some information between them. Client#1 sends a PUT request in order to store some new data that it identifies with a URI path of */objects/2113*. This is a new URI that the REST API has never seen before, meaning that it does not map to any previously stored resource. Therefore, the REST API interprets the request as an *insert* and creates a new resource based on the client's provided state representation and then it returns a 201 ("Created") response.

Some time later, client#2 decides to share some data and it requests the exact same storage URI (*/objects/2113*). Now the REST API *is* able to map this URI to an existing resource, which makes it unclear about the client request's intent. The REST API has not been given enough information to decide whether or not it should overwrite client#1's stored resource state with the new data from client#2. In this scenario, the API is forced to return a 409 ("Conflict") response to client#2's request. The API should also provide some additional information about the error in the response's body.

If client#2 decides to update the stored data, it may retry its request to include the If-Match header. However, if the supplied header value does not match the *current* entity tag value, the REST API must return error code 412 ("Precondition Failed"). If the supplied condition does match, the REST API must update the stored resource's state, and return a 200 ("OK") or 204 ("No Content") response. If the response does include an updated representation of the resource's state, the API must include values for the Last-Modified and ETag headers that reflect the update.

 HTTP supports conditional requests with the GET, POST, and DELETE methods in the same fashion that is illustrated by the example above. This pattern is the key that allows *writable* REST APIs to support collaboration between their clients.

Rule: Location must be used to specify the URI of a newly created resource

The Location response header's value is a URI that identifies a resource that may be of interest to the client. In response to the successful creation of a resource within a collection or store, a REST API must include the Location header to designate the URI of the newly created resource.

In a 202 ("Accepted") response, this header may be used to direct clients to the operational status of an asynchronous controller resource.

Rule: Cache-Control, Expires, and Date response headers should be used to encourage caching

Caching is one of the most useful features built on top of HTTP. You can take advantage of caching to reduce client-perceived latency, to increase reliability, and to reduce the load on an API's servers. Caches can be anywhere. They can be in the API's server network, content delivery networks (CDNs), or the client's network.

When serving a representation, include a Cache-Control header with a max-age value (in seconds) equal to the freshness lifetime. For example:

```
Cache-Control: max-age=60, must-revalidate
```

To support legacy HTTP 1.0 caches, a REST API should include an `Expires` header with the expiration date-time. The value is a time at which the API generated the representation plus the freshness lifetime. REST APIs should also include a `Date` header with a date-time of the time at which the API returned the response. Including this header helps clients compute the freshness lifetime as the difference between the values of the `Expires` and `Date` headers. For example:

```
Date: Tue, 15 Nov 1994 08:12:31 GMT
Expires: Thu, 01 Dec 1994 16:00:00 GMT
```

Rule: Cache-Control, Expires, and Pragma response headers may be used to discourage caching

If a REST API's response must not cached, add `Cache-Control` headers with the value `no-cache` and `no-store`. In this case, also add the `Pragma: no-cache` and `Expires: 0` header values to interoperate with legacy HTTP 1.0 caches.

Rule: Caching should be encouraged

The `no-cache` directive will prevent any cache from serving cached responses. REST APIs should not do this unless absolutely necessary. Using a small value of `max-age` as opposed to adding `no-cache` directive helps clients fetch cached copies for at least a short while without significantly impacting freshness.

Rule: Expiration caching headers should be used with 200 ("OK") responses

Set expiration caching headers in responses to successful `GET` and `HEAD` requests. Although `POST` is cacheable, most caches treat this method as non-cacheable. You need not set expiration headers on other methods.

Rule: Expiration caching headers may optionally be used with 3xx and 4xx responses

In addition to successful responses with the 200 ("OK") response code, consider adding caching headers to 3xx and 4xx responses. Known as *negative caching*, this helps reduce the amount of redirecting and error-triggering load on a REST API.

Rule: Custom HTTP headers must not be used to change the behavior of HTTP methods

You can optionally use custom headers for informational purposes only. Implement clients and servers such that they do not fail when they do not find expected custom headers.

If the information you are conveying through a custom HTTP header is important for the correct interpretation of the request or response, include that information in the body of the request or response or the URI used for the request. Avoid custom headers for such usages.

Media Types

To identify the form of the data contained within a request or response message body, the `Content-Type` header's value references a media type.[*]

Media Type Syntax

Media types have the following syntax:

```
type "/" subtype *( ";" parameter )
```

The *type* value may be one of: `application`, `audio`, `image`, `message`, `model`, `multipart`, `text`, or `video`. A typical REST API will most often work with media types that fall under the `application` type. In a hierarchical fashion, the media type's *subtype* value is subordinate to its *type*.

Note that *parameters* may follow the *type/subtype* in the form of `attribute=value` pairs that are separated by a leading semi-colon (;) character. A media type's specification may designate parameters as either required or optional. Parameter names are case-insensitive. Parameter values are normally case-sensitive and may be enclosed in double quote (" ") characters. When more than one parameter is specified, their ordering is insignificant.

The two examples below demonstrate a `Content-Type` header value that references a media type with a single *charset* parameter:

```
Content-type: text/html; charset=ISO-8859-4
Content-type: text/plain; charset="us-ascii"
```

Registered Media Types

The Internet Assigned Numbers Authority[†] (IANA) governs the set of *registered* media types and provides links to each type's published specification (RFC). The IANA allows anyone to propose a new media type by filling out the "Application for Media Type" form found at *http://www.iana.org/cgi-bin/mediatypes.pl*.

---

[*] Media types were originally known as "MIME types," which stood for Multipurpose Internet Mail Extensions.

[†] *http://www.iana.org/assignments/media-types*

Some commonly used registered media types are listed below:

text/plain
> A plain text format with no specific content structure or markup.‡

text/html
> Content that is formatted using the HyperText Markup Language (HTML).§

image/jpeg
> An image compression method that was standardized by the Joint Photographic Experts Group (JPEG).‖

application/xml
> Content that is structured using the Extensible Markup Language (XML).#

application/atom+xml
> Content that uses the Atom Syndication Format (Atom), which is an XML-based format that structures data into lists known as *feeds*.*

application/javascript
> Source code written in the JavaScript programming language.†

application/json
> The JavaScript Object Notation (JSON) text-based format that is often used by programs to exchange structured data.‡

Vendor-Specific Media Types

Media types use the subtype prefix "vnd" to indicate that they are owned or controlled by a "vendor." Vendor-specific media types convey a clear description of a message's content to the programs that understand their meaning. Unlike their more common counterparts, vendor-specific media types impart application-specific metadata that makes a message more meaningful to the web component that receives it.

Vendor-specific media types may also be registered with the IANA. For example, the following vendor-specific types are among the many listed in the IANA's registry (*http://www.iana.org/assignments/media-types*):

```
application/vnd.ms-excel
application/vnd.lotus-notes
text/vnd.sun.j2me.app-descriptor
```

‡ text/plain (*http://www.rfc-editor.org/rfc/rfc2046.txt*)

§ text/html (*http://www.rfc-editor.org/rfc/rfc2854.txt*)

‖ image/jpeg (*http://www.rfc-editor.org/rfc/rfc2046.txt*)

#application/xml (*http://www.rfc-editor.org/rfc/rfc3023.txt*)

* application/atom+xml (*http://www.rfc-editor.org/rfc/rfc4287.txt*)

† application/javascript (*http://www.rfc-editor.org/rfc/rfc4329.txt*)

‡ application/json (*http://www.rfc-editor.org/rfc/rfc4627.txt*)

Media Type Design

Client developers are encouraged to rely on the *self-descriptive* features of a REST API. In other words, client programs should hardcode as few API-specific details as possible. This goal influences many aspects of a REST API's design, including opaque URIs, hypermedia-based actions with resource state awareness, and descriptive media types.

Rule: Application-specific media types should be used

REST APIs treat the body of an HTTP request or response as part of an application-specific interaction. While the body may be formatted using languages such as JSON or XML, it usually has semantics that require special processing beyond simply parsing the language's syntax.

As an example, consider a REST API URI such as *http://api.soccer.restapi.org/players/2113* that responds to GET requests with a representation of a player resource that is formatted using JSON. If the Content-Type header field value declares that the response's media type is *application/json*, it has accurately conveyed the body content's syntax but has disregarded the semantics and structure of the player representation. The response's Content-Type header simply tells a client that it should expect some JSON-formatted text.

Alternatively, the response's Content-Type header field should communicate that the body contains a representation of a player document that is formatted with JSON. To help achieve this goal, the WRML framework, which was introduced in the section "WRML" on page 7, uses a descriptive media type: *application/wrml*. The example below shows WRML's media type used to describe a player form that is formatted using JSON:

```
# NOTE: the line breaks below are for the sake of visual clarity.

application/wrml;  ❶
    format="http://api.formats.wrml.org/application/json";  ❷
    schema="http://api.schemas.wrml.org/soccer/Player"  ❸
```

❶ The WRML media type.§

❷ The required *format* parameter's value identifies a document resource that describes the JSON format itself.

❸ The required *schema* parameter's value identifies a separate document that details the Player resource type's form, which is independent of the media type's *format* parameter's value.

---

§ The *application/wrml* media type's IANA registration is pending, see *http://www.wrml.org* for the most up-to-date information.

This media type may appear excessive when compared to simpler ones like *application/json*. However, this is a worthwhile trade-off since this media type communicates—*directly to clients*—distinct and complementary bits of information regarding the content of a message. The *application/wrml* media type's self-descriptive and pluggable design reduces the need for information to be communicated out-of-band and then hardcoded by client developers.

 See "Media Type Representation" on page 56, which describes how this media type's format and schema documents should be represented.

Media Type Format Design

Most media types identify a format using a simple string, like *application/json*. Instead, by using a `format` parameter with a URI value, the WRML media type directs client programs to a *cacheable* document that provides links to other documents related to the format. In the example above, the representation of the document referenced by the `format` parameter (*http://api.formats.wrml.org/application/json*) contains links to related web resources, such as *http://www.json.org* and *http://www.rfc-editor.org/rfc/rfc4627.txt*.

More importantly, by leveraging REST's code-on-demand constraint, the format document's representation can provide links to formatting and parsing *code*, which clients can download and execute to serialize and deserialize an HTTP message body's content. By providing this code, available for various programming languages and runtime environments, an API can programmatically teach its clients how to interoperate with its representation formats. The *future-proof* nature of this design may prove especially useful when a REST API wishes to adopt a new format that is not yet widely supported by its clients.

The section "Rule: A consistent form should be used to represent media type formats" on page 56, outlines the structure of a format document's representation.

Media Type Schema Design

As discussed next in Chapter 5, a resource's state representation consists of fields and links. For a given "class" of resource, the set of expected fields and context-sensitive links can be described by a *schema* document. The WRML media type's *schema* parameter references a *cacheable* schema document, which describes a resource type's fields and links; independent of any specific representational format. This separation of concerns allows multiple representation formats to be negotiated by clients and supported by REST APIs with relative ease. With a set of standard *primitive types*, outlined in "Field Representation" on page 60, a schema document can describe a resource representation's fields in a format-independent manner.

The section "Rule: A consistent form should be used to represent media type schemas" on page 59, details the structure of a schema document's representation.

Media Type Schema Versioning

The different *versions* of a given schema should be organized as different schema documents, with distinct URIs. This design is borrowed from the approach traditionally used by the W3C[||] and IETF[#] for *versioning* the URIs of *Internet Drafts* on their way to becoming approved standards. The example below shows the URI of a schema document that details the fields and links of a soccer `Player` resource type:

```
http://api.schemas.wrml.org/soccer/Player-2
```

The `-2` suffix designates the version number of the `Player` resource type's schema. As a rule, the current version of the resource type's schema should always be made available through a separate resource identifier, without a numeric suffix. The example below demonstrates the design of the `Player` resource type's current schema URI:

```
http://api.schemas.wrml.org/soccer/Player
```

The URI of a resource type's current schema version *always* identifies the concept of the most recent version. A schema document URI that ends with a number permanently identifies a specific version of the schema. Therefore the latest version of a schema is always modeled by two separate resources which *conceptually overlap* while the numbered version is also the current one. This overlap results in the two distinct resources, with two separate URIs, consistently having the same state representation.

Rule: Media type negotiation should be supported when multiple representations are available

Allow clients to negotiate for a given format and schema by submitting an `Accept` header with the desired media type. For example:

```
# NOTE: the line breaks below are for the sake of visual clarity.

Accept:  application/wrml;
              format="http://api.formats.wrml.org/text/html";   ❶
              schema="http://api.schemas.wrml.org/soccer/Team"   ❷
```

❶ Using *media type negotiation* clients can select a format.

❷ Using *media type negotiation* clients can select the schema version that will work best for them.

|| World Wide Web Consortium (W3C), *http://www.w3.org*.

\#The Internet Engineering Task Force (IETF), *http://www.ietf.org*.

Additionally, to facilitate browser-based viewing and debugging of a REST API's responses, consider supporting *raw* media types as shown in the example below:

```
Accept: application/json
```

This will allow web browser add-ons such as *JSONView (http://jsonview.com)* to render a REST API's responses as JSON.

Rule: Media type selection using a query parameter may be supported

To enable simple links and easy debugging, REST APIs may support media type selection via a query parameter named *accept* with a value format that mirrors that of the Accept HTTP request header. For example:

```
GET /bookmarks/mikemassedotcom?accept=application/xml
```

This is a more precise and generic approach to media type identification that should be preferred over the common alternative of appending a virtual file extension like *.xml* to the URI's path. The *virtual* file extension approach binds the resource and its representation together, implying that they are one and the same.

 Media type selection (or negotiation) via a query parameter is a form of *tunneling* that conveys metadata in the URI rather than in HTTP's intended slot: the Accept header. Therefore it should be used with careful consideration.

Recap

This chapter covered the design rules for a REST API's metadata conveyed through HTTP headers and media types. Table 4-1 summarizes the vocabulary terms that were used in this chapter.

Table 4-1. Vocabulary review

Term	Description
Atom Syndication Format (Atom)	An XML-based format that structures data into lists known as "feeds."
Conditional request	A client-initiated interaction with a precondition that the server is expected to honor.
Entity	An HTTP request or response payload, which is metadata in header fields and content in a body.
Entity tag	An opaque string value that designates the "version" of a given HTTP response message's headers and body.
Extensible Markup Language (XML)	A standardized application profile of SGML that is used by many applications to exchange data.
Internet Assigned Numbers Authority (IANA)	The entity with many governance-related duties, which include overseeing global IP address allocation and media type registration.
Media type negotiation	A client-initiated process that selects the form of a response message's representation.

Term	Description
Media type schema	A Web-oriented description of a form that is composed of fields and links.
Negative caching	Directing intermediaries to serve copies of responses that did *not* result in a 2xx status code.
Vendor-specific media type	A form descriptor that is owned and controlled by a specific organization.

Table 4-2 recaps a REST API's use of the HTTP headers.

Table 4-2. HTTP response header summary

Code	Purpose
Content-Type	Identifies the entity body's media type
Content-Length	The size (in bytes) of the entity body
Last-Modified	The date-time of last resource representation's change
ETag	Indicates the version of the response message's entity
Cache-Control	A TTL-based caching value (in seconds)
Location	Provides the URI of a resource

## CHAPTER 5

Representation Design

Message Body Format

A REST API commonly uses a response message's entity body to help convey the state of a request message's identified resource. REST APIs often employ a text-based format to represent a resource state as a set of meaningful fields. Today, the most commonly used text formats are XML and JSON.

XML, like HTML, organizes a document's information by nesting angle-bracketed[*] tag pairs. Well-formed XML must have tag pairs that *match* perfectly. This "buddy system" of tag pairs is XML's way of holding a document's structure together.

JSON uses curly brackets[†] to hierarchically structure a document's information. Most programmers are accustomed to this style of scope expression, which makes the JSON format feel natural to folks that are oriented to think in terms of object-based structures.

 This chapter's examples favor the JSON format. However, JSON does not support *invisible* comments or wrapping long string values, which made it difficult to keep some of the examples well-formed. The malformed examples are noted as such inline.

Rule: JSON should be supported for resource representation

As a format for data exchange, JSON supports lightweight and simple interoperation: it does its job. Today, JSON is a popular format that is commonly used in REST API design, much like bell-bottomed jeans were fashionable in the 1970s. JSON borrows some of JavaScript's good parts and benefits from seamless integration with the browser's native runtime environment. If there is not already a standard format for a given resource type (e.g., *image/jpeg* for JPEG-compressed image resources), a REST API should use the JSON format to structure its information.

---

[*] *Angle brackets:* < and >

[†] *Curly brackets:* { and }

This rule is in regard to the JSON data format only and does not necessarily imply that the *application/json* media type should be used as the value of an HTTP message's Content-Type header (see the section "Rule: Application-specific media types should be used" on page 41).

Rule: JSON must be well-formed

A JSON object is an unordered set of name-value pairs. The JSON object syntax defines names as strings which are always surrounded by double quotes. Note that this is a less lenient formatting rule than that of object literals in JavaScript, and this difference often leads to malformed JSON.

The following example shows well-formed JSON with all names enclosed in double quotes.

```
{
    "firstName" : "Osvaldo",
    "lastName" : "Alonso",
    "firstNamePronunciation" : "ahs-VAHL-doe",
    "number" : 6,  ❶
    "birthDate" : "1985-11-11"  ❷
}
```

❶ JSON supports number values directly, so they do not need to be treated as strings.

❷ JSON does not support date-time values, so they are typically formatted as strings.

 Some browsers may *display* a JSON pair's name without the quotes, even though the REST API's response correctly included them.

JSON names should use mixed lower case and should avoid special characters whenever possible. In JavaScript, JSON names like *fooBar* are preferred since they allow the use of the cleaner *dot notation* for property access. For example:

```
var.fooBar
```

Names like *foo-bar* require the use of JavaScript's less elegant bracket notation to access the property, such as:

```
var["foo-bar"]
```

Rule: XML and other formats may optionally be used for resource representation

The section "Rule: JSON should be supported for resource representation" on page 47, established that JSON should be a supported representation format for clients. REST APIs may optionally support XML, HTML, and other languages as alternative formats for resource representation. Clients should express their desired representation using media type negotiation as described in "Rule: Media type negotiation should be supported when multiple representations are available" on page 43.

The format-neutral nature of WRML's schemas, introduced in "Media Type Schema Design" on page 42, enable the same consistently structured form to be presented using a variety of markup and formatting languages. For example, a document might be formatted using JSON or XML so that it can be easily inspected by a client or server program. The same document could be rendered using HTML and CSS when viewed in a browser, so that schemas may also take on the job of documenting a REST API's structures for client developers. Furthermore, using JavaScript, a browser-rendered document can offer an HTML form that allows interactive editing of the document's form fields.

Rule: Additional envelopes must not be created

A REST API must leverage the message "envelope" provided by HTTP. In other words, the body should contain a representation of the resource state, without any additional, transport-oriented wrappers.

Hypermedia Representation

Much like the Web's HTML-based hyperlinks (links) and forms, REST APIs employ hypermedia within representations. A REST API response message's body includes links to indicate the associations and actions that are available for a given resource, in a given state. Included along with other fields of a resource's state representation, links convey the relationships between resources and offer clients a menu of resource-related actions, which are context-sensitive.

On the Web, users click on links to navigate a universe of interconnected resources. Despite the Web's ever-increasing number of diverse resources, a few simple and uniformly structured HTML elements convey everything the browser needs to know in order to facilitate navigation. Similarly, REST API clients can programmatically navigate using a uniform link structure.

The following rules present WRML's solution for representing the link and link relation structures.

Rule: A consistent form should be used to represent links

The structure detailed in this rule represents a single link. Links should be included, along with fields, within resource state representations. A single link does not typically stand alone as a request or response message body's content. However for completeness sake, the media type for the link structure is defined below:

```
# NOTE: the line breaks below are for the sake of visual clarity.

application/wrml;  ❶
    format="http://api.formats.wrml.org/application/json";
    schema="http://api.schemas.wrml.org/common/Link"  ❷
```

❶ The WRML media type.

❷ Identifies the current version of the Link schema.

When formatted with JSON, a Link representation has the following consistent form:

```
{
    "href" : Text <constrained by URI or URI Template syntax>,  ❶
    "rel"  : Text <constrained by URI syntax>,  ❷
    "requestTypes"  : Array <constrained to contain media type text elements>,  ❸
    "responseTypes" : Array <constrained to contain media type text elements>,  ❹
    "title" : Text  ❺
}
```

❶ The required href value identifies the link's target resource. The value may be either a URI or a URI template. A URI template with path-based variables should only be used with links that use PUT to *insert* a resource into a store. URI templates with query-based variables may be used more generally.

❷ The required *rel* value identifies a document that describes the link's relation (see "Rule: A consistent form should be used to represent link relations" on page 52).

❸ The optional requestTypes value is an array that lists the linked resource's allowed request body media types. This field tells clients what types of inputs are allowed by the link. Clients are encouraged to consult this list before issuing PUT or POST requests to the linked resource. If present, this value takes precedence over the field with the same name that is defined by the link's relation document.

❹ The optional responseTypes value is an array that lists the linked resource's available response body media types. This field tells clients what types of outputs may be returned by the link. Clients are encouraged to consult this list to help prioritize media types in the Accept header of requests to the linked resource. If present, this value takes precedence over the field with the same name that is defined by the link's relation document.

❺ The optional *title* value provides a plain text title for the specific link.

Below is an example of a link with the minimum required set of fields:

```
{
    "href" : "http://api.soccer.restapi.org/players/2113",  ❶
    "rel"  : "http://api.relations.wrml.org/common/self"  ❷
}
```

❶ The link's *href* value identifies the target resource.

❷ The link's *rel* value identifies a document that describes the commonly used *self* link relation. The self relation signifies that the *href* identifies a resource equivalent to the containing resource.

The example below shows the same link with some optional fields included. This example also illustrates a use of the media types discussed in "Media Type Design" on page 41:

```
# NOTE: the line breaks in the responseTypes array's string values are
# not allowed, but they are necessary for the book's formatting. JSON does
# not provide support for line continuation.

{
    "href" : "http://api.soccer.restapi.org/players/2113",
    "rel"  : "http://api.relations.wrml.org/common/self",
    "responseTypes" : [  ❶
        "application/wrml;
         format=\"http://api.formats.wrml.org/application/json\";  ❷
         schema=\"http://api.schemas.wrml.org/soccer/Player\"",   ❸

        "application/wrml;
         format=\"http://api.formats.wrml.org/application/xml\";
         schema=\"http://api.schemas.wrml.org/soccer/Player\"",

        "application/wrml;
         format=\"http://api.formats.wrml.org/text/html\";
         schema=\"http://api.schemas.wrml.org/soccer/Player\"",

        "application/json",  ❹
        "application/xml",
        "text/html"
    ],
    "title" : "Osvaldo Alonso"
}
```

❶ The link's `responseTypes` value lists the linked resource's available response body media types. Note that although the WRML media type includes URIs in its `format` and `schema` parameters, they are not intended to be used as hypermedia links in this context.

❷ The media type's `format` parameter identifies a document that describes the JSON format. See "Media Type Format Design" on page 42 for more information.

❸ The media type's `schema` parameter identifies the current version of the `Player` schema.

❹ The common media types are supported for viewers that don't care about the data's semantics.

Rule: A consistent form should be used to represent link relations

Every link has a *rel* value to identify a document that describes the link's relation. A link's *rel* value describes the relationship from the current resource to the resource specified by the link's *href* attribute. Link relations tell clients how to interact with links. The IANA provides a registry (*http://www.iana.org/assignments/link-relations/link-rela tions.xml*) for common link relations.

When formatted with JSON, a LinkRelation has the following media type:

```
# NOTE: the line breaks below are for the sake of visual clarity.

application/wrml;  ❶
    format="http://api.formats.wrml.org/application/json";
    schema="http://api.schemas.wrml.org/common/LinkRelation"  ❷
```

❶ The WRML media type.

❷ Identifies the current version of the LinkRelation resource type's schema.

When represented using JSON, a LinkRelation has the following consistent structure:

```
{
    "name"     : Text,  ❶
    "method" : Text <constrained to be choice of HTTP method>,  ❷
    "requestTypes"  : Array <constrained to contain media type text elements>,  ❸
    "responseTypes" : Array <constrained to contain media type text elements>,  ❹
    "description"    : Text,  ❺
    "title"  : Text   ❻
}
```

❶ The required name value conveys the link relation's name. Link relations should be name using mixed lower case.

❷ The optional method value designates the HTTP method that is associated with the link relation. If this field is omitted, the GET HTTP method must be assumed.

❸ The optional requestTypes value is an array that lists the link relation's allowed request body media types. Clients are encouraged to consult this list before issuing PUT or POST requests to a linked resource. This value should be specified whenever the list of allowed media types are known to *always* be associated with a link relation.

❹ The optional responseTypes value is an array that lists the link relation's available response body media types. Clients are encouraged to consult this list to help prioritize media types in the Accept header of requests to a linked resource. This value should be specified whenever the list of available media types are known to *always* be associated with a link relation.

❺ The required description value provides a plain text description of the link relation. Link relation document representations may also contain links to other resources, such as human-readable documentation (see "Rule: A consistent form should be used to advertise links" on page 53).

❻ The optional *title* value provides a plain text title for the link relation.

Below is an example of an HTTP request and response for a link relation document:

```
# Request
GET /common/self HTTP/1.1
Host: api.relations.wrml.org

# Response
HTTP/1.1 200 OK
Content-Type: application/wrml;
             format="http://api.formats.wrml.org/application/json";
             schema="http://api.schemas.wrml.org/common/LinkRelation"

# NOTE: The description's line breaks must be omitted in well-formed JSON.
{
    "name"    : "self",
    "method" : "GET",  ❶
    "description" : "Signifies that the URI in the value of the href  ❷
                    property identifies a resource equivalent to the
                    containing resource."
}
```

❶ The *self* link relation tells clients how to retrieve a resource.

❷ This text is wrapped due to the book's format only. JSON does not allow line continuation, which means this string is malformed.

 Link relation document representations are designed to be *cacheable*, thus the response headers should encourage clients to do so (see "Rule: Cache-Control, Expires, and Date response headers should be used to encourage caching" on page 37).

Rule: A consistent form should be used to advertise links

On its own, the uniform link structure is insufficient to enable clients to programmatically find and process a representation's hypermedia. A REST API must also offer clients a consistent way to easily discover the available links within a representation. To enable this, representations should include a structure, named links, to contain all of the links that are available in the resource's current state. The links structure is a predictable place for clients to easily look up known links, by their simple relation names, as well as discover new links.

The following example shows how the consistent links structure appears when formatted using JSON:

```
{
  "firstName" : "Osvaldo",
  "lastName" : "Alonso",
  "links" : {  ❶
    "self" : {
      "href" : "http://api.soccer.restapi.org/players/2113",
```

```
        "rel"   : "http://api.relations.wrml.org/common/self"
      },
      "parent" : {
        "href"  : "http://api.soccer.restapi.org/players",
        "rel"   : "http://api.relations.wrml.org/common/parent"
      },
      "team"   : {  ❷
        "href"  : "http://api.soccer.restapi.org/teams/seattle",
        "rel"   : "http://api.relations.wrml.org/soccer/team"
      },
      "addToFavorites" : {
        "href"  : "http://api.soccer.restapi.org/users/42/favorites/{name}",   ❸
        "rel"   : "http://api.relations.wrml.org/common/addToFavorites"
      }
    }
  }
}
```

❶ The links field is a *top-level* name-value pair in each JSON object. Each of the links object's fields must conform to the uniform link structure.

❷ Link relation names like *team* can be efficiently looked up by clients using JSON libraries that deserialize objects into map or associative array data structures. These link relations are an important part of a REST API's "vocabulary." Client developers may treat the names of a REST API's link relations as application-specific *keywords* that may be hardcoded in clients. In contrast, client developers should *not* hardcode the URIs of the link relation documents.

❸ To support a client's ability to add a resource to a store, a REST API may use a URI template that contains path-based variables as the value of a link's *href*. In this simple example, the client must supply a *name* for the "favorite" to add, possibly by prompting a user for it.

Rule: A self link should be included in response message body representations

A response message body that contains a representation of an identifiable resource should include a link named *self*. The self link relation signifies that the *href* value identifies a resource equivalent to the containing resource. See "Rule: A consistent form should be used to advertise links" on page 53 for an example.

Rule: Minimize the number of advertised "entry point" API URIs

When looking at the Web for REST API design direction, we should consider the ubiquity of the home page concept and its associated site navigation. The REST API equivalent is to provide human-readable documentation that advertises the URI of the API's docroot. The docroot's representation should provide links to make every other resource programmatically available.

API documentation that advertises the service's individual resource URIs, or URI templates, can lead client developers to code tightly coupled clients that do not treat the API's URIs as opaque identifiers. Instead, client developers should be instructed to make use of the API's hypermedia.

Rule: Links should be used to advertise a resource's available actions in a state-sensitive manner

Web APIs commonly rely on accompanying human-readable documentation to advertise the actions that can be performed on its various resources. Typically, this documentation simply lists each URI template and describes the expected outcome associated with each client interaction. This approach to conveying the application-specific protocol falls down in three key ways:

1. It is insensitive to the state of resources, leaving it up to the client developers to determine which resource interactions are appropriate for a given application state.

2. It is out-of-band information that is available to the client developer rather than the client program itself.

3. It leads to hardcoded and tightly coupled clients, which may limit the API's ability to evolve over time without breaking its existing clients.

REST's HATEOAS[‡] constraint specifies that an API must answer all client requests with resource representations that contain *state-sensitive* links. The following example shows hypermedia used to model the state of an application's "Edit" menu's actions:

```
{
    # Fields...

    "links" : {
        "self" : {
            "href" : "http://api.editor.restapi.org/docs/48679",
            "rel"  : "http://api.relations.wrml.org/common/self"
        },
        "cut" : {
            "href" : "http://api.editor.restapi.org/docs/48679/edit/cut",
            "rel"  : "http://api.relations.wrml.org/editor/edit/cut"
        },
        "copy" : {
            "href" : "http://api.editor.restapi.org/docs/48679/edit/copy",
            "rel"  : "http://api.relations.wrml.org/editor/edit/copy"
        }
    }
}
```

‡ HATEOAS is an acronym for "Hypermedia as the Engine of Application State."

Continuing with this example, imagine that the application has a server-side "Clipboard" resource that enables clients to share data. If, at some point, the Clipboard's state allows the client to retrieve its data, the REST API will make a *paste* link available. The example below shows that the client's "Paste" menu item and toolbar button widgets should now be enabled; however, the server-managed "selection" state of the edited resource is now empty so there is currently nothing to *cut* or *copy*.

```
{
    # Fields...

    "links" : {
        "self" : {
            "href" : "http://api.editor.restapi.org/docs/48679",
            "rel"  : "http://api.relations.wrml.org/common/self"
        },
        "paste" : {
            "href" : "http://api.editor.restapi.org/docs/48679/edit/paste",
            "rel"  : "http://api.relations.wrml.org/editor/edit/paste"
        }
    }
}
```

Media Type Representation

The *application/wrml* media type, introduced in "Media Type Design" on page 41, has two parameters: *format* and *schema*. These parameters have URI values that reference separate documents, each of which can enhance the semantics of the metadata attached to the Content-Type and Accept HTTP headers. This section's rules describe the representations of these two document types.

Rule: A consistent form should be used to represent media type formats

Unlike traditional media types like *application/json* and *application/xml*, the *application/wrml* media type stipulates a *format* parameter with a URI value to address a document that describes the format of some content.

When formatted with JSON, a Format has the following media type:

```
# NOTE: the line breaks below are for the sake of visual clarity.

application/wrml;  ❶
    format="http://api.formats.wrml.org/application/json";  ❷
    schema="http://api.schemas.wrml.org/common/Format"  ❸
```

❶ The WRML media type.

❷ Identifies the format of the format document, which in this JSON-based example would be equivalent to the format's *self* link's value (see "Rule: A self link should be included in response message body representations" on page 54).

❸ Identifies the current version of the Format resource type's schema.

When represented using JSON, a `Format` has the following consistent structure:

```
{
    "mediaType" : Text <constrained by media type syntax>,   ❶
    "links" : {
        "home" : Link <form constrained by the Link schema>, ❷
        "rfc"  : Link <form constrained by the Link schema>  ❸
    },
    "serialize" : {   ❹
        "links" : {
            <Set of Link schema-constrained forms>
        }
    },
    "deserialize" : {   ❺
        "links" : {
            <Set of Link schema-constrained forms>
        }
    }
}
```

❶ The required `mediaType` value uniquely identifies the format.

❷ The optional `home` link's `href` identifies the format's home page resource.

❸ The optional `rfc` link's `href` identifies the format's RFC resource.

❹ The optional `serialize` section categorizes links into platform-specific code that clients may download and execute to marshall a runtime's structures into the format.

❺ The optional `deserialize` structure groups links into platform-specific code that clients may download and execute to unmarshall formatted content into runtime structures.

Below is an example of an HTTP request and response for the JSON format document's representation:

```
# Request
GET /application/json HTTP/1.1
Host: api.formats.wrml.org

# Response
HTTP/1.1 200 OK
Content-Type: application/wrml;
              format="http://api.formats.wrml.org/application/json";
              schema="http://api.schemas.wrml.org/common/Format"

{
  "mediaType" : "application/json", ❶
  "links" : {
    "self" : {
      "href" : "http://api.formats.wrml.org/application/json",
      "rel"  : "http://api.relations.wrml.org/common/self"
    },
    "home" : {
      "href" : "http://www.json.org",
      "rel"  : "http://api.relations.wrml.org/common/home"
```

```
      },
      "rfc" : {
        "href" : "http://www.rfc-editor.org/rfc/rfc4627.txt",
        "rel"  : "http://api.relations.wrml.org/format/rfc"
      }
    },
    "serialize" : {
      "links" : {
        "java" : {  ❷
          "href" : "http://api.formats.wrml.org/application/json/serializers/java",
          "rel"  : "http://api.relations.wrml.org/format/serialize/java"
        },
        "php" : {  ❸
          "href" : "http://api.formats.wrml.org/application/json/serializers/php",
          "rel"  : "http://api.relations.wrml.org/format/serialize/php"
        }
      }
    },
    "deserialize" : {
      "links" : {
        "java" : {  ❹
          "href" : "http://api.formats.wrml.org/application/json/deserializers/java",
          "rel"  : "http://api.relations.wrml.org/format/deserialize/java"
        },
        "perl" : {  ❺
          "href" : "http://api.formats.wrml.org/application/json/deserializers/perl",
          "rel"  : "http://api.relations.wrml.org/format/deserialize/perl"
        }
      }
    }
  }
}
```

❶ The mediaType value identifies the JSON format.

❷ The java link references a Java Archive (JAR) containing compiled code that conforms to a standard serializer interface.

❸ The php link references executable PHP code that conforms to a standard serializer interface.

❹ The java link references a JAR containing compiled code that conforms to a standard deserializer interface.

❺ The perl link references executable Perl code that conforms to a standard deserializer interface.

 Format document representations are designed to be *cacheable*, thus the response headers should encourage clients to do so (see "Rule: Cache-Control, Expires, and Date response headers should be used to encourage caching" on page 37).

Rule: A consistent form should be used to represent media type schemas

Programmers working with the Web are familiar with modeling informational in multiple domains and formats. For example, it is common to model a data structure's *fields* as: database columns, class properties, and web page template variables. A REST API uses resource-oriented *schemas* to describe the structure of its representations independent of their format. By exposing to clients a separate, format-agnostic schema resource for each of its distinct resource types, a REST API can present a dynamic and discoverable interface. Schemas provide contractual resource type definitions, which are a crucial component of the interface that binds a REST API and its clients together.

In object-oriented terms, a structured *representational form*, which is carried by an individual HTTP request or response message body, is analogous to an *instance* of a schema *class*. A representational form, or just *form* for short, consists of the fields and links as detailed by the "blueprints" of its associated schema document.

This rule presents the representation of schemas, and their related components, which a REST API may use to describe its various forms.

Schema Representation

When formatted with JSON, a `Schema` has the following media type:

```
# NOTE: the line breaks below are for the sake of visual clarity.

application/wrml;  ❶
    format="http://api.formats.wrml.org/application/json";
    schema="http://api.schemas.wrml.org/common/Schema"  ❷
```

❶ The WRML media type.

❷ Identifies the current version of the `Schema` resource type's schema.

When represented using JSON, a `Schema` has the following consistent form:

```
{
    "name" : Text <constrained to be mixed uppercase>,  ❶
    "version" : Integer,  ❷
    "extends" : Array <constrained to contain (schema) URI text elements>,  ❸
    "fields" : {  ❹
        <Set of Field schema-constrained forms>
    },
    "stateFacts" : Array <constrained to contain mixed uppercase text elements>,  ❺
    "linkFormulas" : {  ❻
        <Set of LinkFormula schema-constrained forms>
    },
    "description" : Text  ❼
}
```

❶ The required `name` value declares the schema's mixed uppercase name, which includes no whitespace and capitalizes the first character of each word.

❷ The required `version` value is a one-based integer that indicates the schema's revision number.

❸ The optional `extends` value lists the URIs that identify the schema's base schemas. Schema extension allows a schema's forms to inherit the fields and links of its base schemas. Schema extension is analogous to the interface inheritance model offered by classical object-oriented programming languages like Java and C#.

❹ The optional `fields` structure contains the schema's field definitions (see "Field Representation" on page 60).

❺ The optional `stateFacts` value lists each discrete condition that contributes to a form's potential state. Each state fact is a text-based identifier, which by convention is named using mixed uppercase. A schema's state fact values are used as Boolean variable-based operands within its link formulas.

❻ The optional `linkFormulas` structure contains the schema's link formulas (see "Link Formula Representation" on page 63).

❼ An optional plain text description of the schema.

Field Representation

A schema *field* is a named slot with some associated information that is stored in its value. Each field's value may be one of the following types:

Boolean
> A `Boolean` field's value is either *true* or *false*. Formats lacking support for `Boolean` values must use the text-based literal values: "true" and "false."

Choice
> A `Choice` is a special text-based value that is selected from a static menu of possible text literals. This type is similar to an enumeration (*enum*) in languages like Java and C#. The `Choice` field's available selections is determined by the required `Menu` constraint, as described in "Constraint Representation" on page 62.

DateTime
> Used for date and time-related data. Formats lacking support for `DateTime` values must use the text-based ISO 8601 format enclosed in double quotes.

Double
> A 64-bit IEEE 754 floating point number. Formats lacking support for `Double` values should enclose the value in double quotes (e.g., "3.14159265").

Integer
> A 32-bit signed two's complement integer, like Java's *int*, except that the octal and hexadecimal formats are not used. Formats lacking support for `Integer` values should enclose the integer value in double quotes (e.g., "42").

List
> An linearly ordered group of homogeneous elements with zero-based indices. The homogeneity of a `List` field is determined by an `ElementType` constraint, as described in "Constraint Representation" on page 62.

Schema
> A special text-based value that contains a schema's URI (e.g., "http://api.schemas.wrml.org/soccer/Player"). Schema-typed fields are used to indicate that the representational form's field will contain a structure that complies with the specified schema. For example, in JSON, the field's named value should be an object that conforms to the structure of the field's referenced schema.

Text
> A sequence of zero or more Unicode characters, enclosed in double quotes, using backslash escapes.

null
> The literal `null` is not a field type but rather it acts as a blank value for any field type. Formats lacking support for `null` (or `NULL`) values must use the text-based literal value "null" instead.

An individual field is not typically transferred within a request or response message body. However, when formatted with JSON, a `Field` has the following media type:

```
# NOTE: the line breaks below are for the sake of visual clarity.

application/wrml;  ❶
    format="http://api.formats.wrml.org/application/json";
    schema="http://api.schemas.wrml.org/common/Field"  ❷
```

❶ The WRML media type.

❷ Identifies the current version of the `Field` resource type's schema.

When represented using JSON, a `Field` has the following consistent form:

```
{
    "type" : Text <constrained to be one of the primitive field types>,  ❶
    "defaultValue" : <a type-specific value>,  ❷
    "readOnly" : Boolean,  ❸
    "required" : Boolean,  ❹
    "hidden"   : Boolean,  ❺
    "constraints" : Array <constrained to contain (constraint) URI text elements>,  ❻
    "description" : Text  ❼
}
```

❶ The required `type` value is constrained to be one of these options: "Boolean," "Choice," "DateTime," "Double," "Integer," "List," "Schema," or "Text."

❷ The optional `defaultValue` is a type-specific value that varies according to the field's type. If no default value is specified, each form's corresponding field value will default to *null*.

❸ The optional `readOnly` Boolean flag value indicates whether clients are allowed to specify a value for the field within a representation carried by a request message's body.

❹ The optional `required` Boolean flag value indicates whether a value for this field is required when a client submits its containing form to a REST API.

❺ The optional `hidden` Boolean flag value indicates whether a REST API should include the field within forms carried by its response messages.

❻ The optional `constraints` value lists the field's constraint references (see "Constraint Representation" on page 62).

❼ An optional plain text description of the field.

Schema extension may be used to alter the metadata associated with an inherited field. For example, a *subschema* can *override* a base schema's field by defining one with its exact same name. The subschema may then set the field's *hidden* flag value to *true*, which effectively defines a form type without the field. Using extension to introduce such slight schema variations may be worthwhile in cases where a certain class of clients (e.g., mobile applications) consistently desire a "trimmed" representation of a resource's state.

Constraint Representation

A schema field's *constraints* value lists the URIs of the constraints that are applied to a form's associated field value. A *constraint* restricts a field's possible values. Common constraints include:

- A range constraint that restricts the value of a field to fall between some specific minimum and maximum values.
- A `Choice` field's `Menu` constraint, which limits the value's options to a predefined set of text literals.
- A `List` field's `ElementType` constraint, which enforces the homogeneous nature of its elements.
- A `Text` field constraint used to ensure that its value adheres to a specific syntax (e.g., URI, URI template, regex pattern, etc.)

When formatted with JSON, a `Constraint` has the following media type:

```
# NOTE: the line breaks below are for the sake of visual clarity.

application/wrml;  ❶
    format="http://api.formats.wrml.org/application/json";
    schema="http://api.schemas.wrml.org/common/Constraint"  ❷
```

❶ The WRML media type.

❷ Identifies the current version of the `Constraint` resource type's schema.

When represented using JSON, a `Constraint` has the following consistent structure:

```
{
    "name"     : Text,    ❶
    "validate" : {        ❷
        "links" : {
            <Set of Link schema-constrained forms>
        }
    }
}
```

❶ The required `name` value declares the constraint's mixed uppercase name, which includes no whitespace and capitalizes the first character of each word.

❷ A constraint may be enforced by both a REST API and its clients by downloading and executing the referenced code that conforms to a per-platform validation interface.

Link Formula Representation

A schema *link formula* equates the availability of a state-sensitive link in a response message body's form with a Boolean expression that uses the schema's state facts as operands. For example, a soccer `Game` form might include a link to its associated `Recap` resource only after the game is over and its final score is known. This state could be indicated with a state fact named *Final*, which would only be *true* once the game is over. Link formulas enable REST APIs to utilize a simple HATEOAS-oriented calculator that executes the formula's Boolean expression to determine if a form should include a particular link.

The following link formulas exemplify how state facts can act as reusable operands:

```
self = Identifiable  ❶
parent = Identifiable and not Docroot  ❷
update = Identifiable and not ReadOnly  ❸
recap = Final  ❹
scoreboard = InProgress or Final  ❺
```

❶ The `self` link should be included in any form that is associated with an identifiable resource.

❷ The `parent` link should be included in every identifiable resource representation; except the REST API's docroot, which by definition has no parent resource.

❸ The `update` link should be included in all representations of identifiable and mutable resources.

❹ The `recap` link should be included in a `Game` form once the game is final.

❺ The `scoreboard` link should be included in a `Game` form if the game is currently in progress or has already ended.

Link formulas are contained by schema structures. Therefore, they are not typically singled out within a request or response message's body. However, for uniformity's sake, when formatted with JSON, a `LinkFormula` has the following media type:

```
# NOTE: the line breaks below are for the sake of visual clarity.

application/wrml;  ❶
    format="http://api.formats.wrml.org/application/json";
    schema="http://api.schemas.wrml.org/common/LinkFormula"  ❷
```

❶ The WRML media type.

❷ Identifies the current version of the `LinkFormula` resource type's schema.

When represented using JSON, a `LinkFormula` has the following consistent form:

```
{
    "rel"  : Text <constrained by URI syntax>,  ❶
    "condition" : Text <constrained to be a state fact-based Boolean expression>  ❷
}
```

❶ The required `rel` value identifies a document that describes a link relation (see "Rule: A consistent form should be used to represent link relations" on page 52).

❷ The required `condition` value is a Boolean expression that uses the schema's state facts as operands.

Automating a REST API implementation's HATEOAS using link formulas is discussed further in Chapter 7.

Document Schema Representation

As mentioned earlier in "Document" on page 15, `Document` is the base form for all resource types. Below is an example of an HTTP request and response for the `Document` schema resource's representation:

```
# Request
GET /common/Document HTTP/1.1
Host: api.schemas.wrml.org

# Response
HTTP/1.1 200 OK
Content-Type: application/wrml;
              format="http://api.formats.wrml.org/application/json";
              schema="http://api.schemas.wrml.org/common/Document"

{
    "name" : "Document",
    "version" : 1,
    "stateFacts" : ["Docroot", "Identifiable", "ReadOnly"],  ❶
    "linkFormulas" : {  ❷
        "self" : {
            "rel" : "http://api.relations.wrml.org/common/self",
            "condition" : "Identifiable"  ❸
        },
```

```
            "metadata" : {
                "rel" : "http://api.relations.wrml.org/common/metadata",  ❹
                "condition" : "Identifiable"
            },
            "parent" : {
                "rel" : "http://api.relations.wrml.org/common/parent",
                "condition" : "Identifiable and not Docroot"
            },
            "update" : {
                "rel" : "http://api.relations.wrml.org/common/update",
                "condition" : "Identifiable and not ReadOnly"
            },
            "delete" : {
                "rel" : "http://api.relations.wrml.org/common/delete",
                "condition" : "Identifiable and not Docroot"
            }
        },
        "description" : "A resource archetype used to model a singular concept.",
        "links" : {  ❺
            "self" : {
                "href" : "http://api.schemas.wrml.org/common/Document",
                "rel"  : "http://api.relations.wrml.org/common/self"
            }

            # Other common schema links...
        }
    }
}
```

❶ Defines the stateFacts that apply "universally" to all REST API resource types.

❷ Defines the linkFormulas that determine the availability of the common links.

❸ The self link is available for all identifiable forms, which includes all resource representations. Temporary forms such as errors and some controller execution results may not necessarily be identifiable: they have no associated URI.

❹ The metadata link relation describes the use of the HEAD request method to retrieve a resource representation's header values.

❺ Note that, like all other forms, schema representations may contain links that allow them to be manipulated by clients.

Container Schema Representation

As mentioned in "Resource Archetypes" on page 15, a Collection models a server-managed *directory* of resources and a Store is a client-managed resource repository. Below is an example of an HTTP request and response for their common base Container schema resource's representation:

```
# Request
GET /common/Container HTTP/1.1
Host: api.schemas.wrml.org
```

```
# Response
HTTP/1.1 200 OK
Content-Type: application/wrml;
              format="http://api.formats.wrml.org/application/json";
              schema="http://api.schemas.wrml.org/common/Container"

{
  "name" : "Container",
  "version" : 1,
  "extends" : ["http://api.schemas.wrml.org/common/Document"], ❶
  "fields" : {
    "elements" : {  ❷
      "type" : "List",
      "description" : "The paginated list of contained elements."
    },
    "size" : {
      "type" : "Integer",
      "description" : "The total number of elements currently contained."
    },
    "pageSize" : {
      "type" : "Integer",
      "description" : "The maximum number of elements returned per page."
    },
    "pageStartIndex" : {
      "type" : "Integer",
      "description" : "The zero-based index of the page's first element."
    },
  },
  "stateFacts" : [
    "Empty",   ❸
    "FirstPage",
    "LastPage",
    "Paginated"
  ],
  "linkFormulas" : {
    "delete" : {  ❹
      "rel" : "http://api.relations.wrml.org/common/delete",
      "condition" : "Identifiable and not Docroot and Empty"
    },
    "next" : {  ❺
      "rel" : "http://api.relations.wrml.org/common/next",
      "condition" : "(Identifiable and not Empty) and (Paginated and not LastPage)"
    },
    "previous" : {  ❻
      "rel" : "http://api.relations.wrml.org/common/previous",
      "condition" : "(Identifiable and not Empty) and (Paginated and not FirstPage)"
    }
  },
  "description" : "A base container of elements."
}
```

❶ The Container schema extends the base Document schema. Note that if no extends value is specified, inheriting from Document is automatically implied, but it may be explicitly declared as shown here.

---

❷ The elements field is common to both collection and store representational forms.

❸ The Container schema introduces the Empty state fact, which is used to indicate the state of containing zero elements. Note that this schema inherits the Document schema's common state facts.

❹ Resources with schemas derived from Container may be deleted only when empty.

❺ Link formula to advance to the next page.

❻ Link formula to revert to the previous page.

Collection Schema Representation

Below is an example of an HTTP request and response for the Collection schema resource's representation:

```
# Request
GET /common/Collection HTTP/1.1
Host: api.schemas.wrml.org

# Response
HTTP/1.1 200 OK
Content-Type: application/wrml;
            format="http://api.formats.wrml.org/application/json";
            schema="http://api.schemas.wrml.org/common/Collection"

# NOTE: The description's line break must be omitted in well-formed JSON.

{
    "name" : "Collection",
    "version" : 1,
    "extends" : ["http://api.schemas.wrml.org/common/Container"],
    "linkFormulas" : {
        "create" : {
            "rel" : "http://api.relations.wrml.org/common/create",
            "condition" : "Identifiable and not ReadOnly"
        }
    },
    "description" : "A resource archetype used to model a server-managed
                    directory of resources."
}
```

A collection's create link enables new elements to be created and contained, as discussed earlier in "Rule: POST must be used to create a new resource in a collection" on page 26.

Store Schema Representation

Below is an example of an HTTP request and response for the Store schema resource's representation:

```
# Request
GET /common/Store HTTP/1.1
Host: api.schemas.wrml.org

# Response
HTTP/1.1 200 OK
Content-Type: application/wrml;
              format="http://api.formats.wrml.org/application/json";
              schema="http://api.schemas.wrml.org/common/Store"

# NOTE: The description's line break must be omitted in well-formed JSON.

{
    "name" : "Store",
    "version" : 1,
    "extends" : ["http://api.schemas.wrml.org/common/Container"],
    "linkFormulas" : {
        "insert" : {
            "rel" : "http://api.relations.wrml.org/common/insert",
            "condition" : "Identifiable and not ReadOnly"
        }
    },
    "description" : "A resource archetype used to model a client-managed
                    resource repository."
}
```

A store's **insert** link may be used to add a new resource, with a URI specified by the client. To assist clients, a store's representational form should provide a URI template in the link's **href** value. The URI template fully identifies the store itself, while leaving the newly stored resource's name as a variable path segment. For example:

```
"insert" : {
    "href" : "http://api.soccer.restapi.org/users/42/favorites/{name}",
    "rel" : "http://api.relations.wrml.org/common/insert",
}
```

For further explanation, refer back to the section "Rule: PUT must be used to both insert and update a stored resource" on page 25.

Error Representation

As mentioned in Chapter 3, HTTP's **4xx** and **5xx** error status codes should be augmented with client-readable information in the response message's entity body. This section's rules present consistent forms pertaining to errors and error responses.

Rule: A consistent form should be used to represent errors

This rule describes the form of a single error that may be included within a REST API's error response message. For completeness sake, the media type is defined below but would not be used in the response's **Content-Type** header (see "Rule: A consistent form should be used to represent error responses" on page 69 instead):

```
# NOTE: the line breaks below are for the sake of visual clarity.

application/wrml;
    format="http://api.formats.wrml.org/application/json";
    schema="http://api.schemas.wrml.org/common/Error"
```

When formatted with JSON, an Error has the following consistent form:

```
{
    "id" : Text,   ❶
    "description" : Text   ❷
}
```

❶ The unique ID/code of the error type. Clients should use this ID to understand what sort of error has occurred and act/message accordingly.

❷ A optional plain text description of the error.

Rule: A consistent form should be used to represent error responses

A REST API returns the error response representation in the message body when a request results in one or more errors. When using this structure, the response should also have the status code set to something in the 4xx or 5xx range.

When formatted with JSON, an error response has the following media type:

```
# NOTE: the line breaks below are for the sake of visual clarity.

application/wrml;   ❶
    format="http://api.formats.wrml.org/application/json";
    schema="http://api.schemas.wrml.org/common/ErrorContainer"   ❷
```

❶ The WRML media type.

❷ Identifies the current version of the ErrorContainer schema.

When represented using JSON, an ErrorContainer has the following consistent form:

```
{
    "elements" : [   ❶
        {   ❷
            "id" : "Update Failed",
            "description" : "Failed to update /users/1234"
        }
    ]
}
```

❶ Extends the Container schema, which means its forms have a List field (array in JSON) named elements.

❷ The ErrorContainer adds an ElementType constraint that ensures the elements list homogeneously contains only Error forms.

Rule: Consistent error types should be used for common error conditions

Generic error types may be leveraged by a variety of APIs. These error types should be defined once and then shared across all APIs via a service hosting the error schema documents. By leveraging schema extension, as discussed in "Media Type Schema Design" on page 42, APIs may define new error types that extend base types with additional fields.

Recap

This chapter offered design rules for resource representations. Table 5-1 summarizes the vocabulary terms that were used in this chapter.

Table 5-1. Vocabulary review

Term	Description
Field	A named slot with some associated information that is stored in its value.
Form	A structured representation that consists of the fields and links, which are defined by an associated schema.
Format	Describes a form's presentation apart from its schematic.
Link	An actionable reference to a resource.
Link formula	A boolean expression that may serve as HATEOAS calculator's input in order to determine the availability of state-sensitive hypermedia within a form.
Link relation	Describes a connection between two resources.
Schema	Describes a representational form's structure independent of its format.
State fact	A Boolean variable that communicates a condition that is relevant to some state-sensitive hypermedia.

## CHAPTER 6

Client Concerns

Introduction

Any computer program can be a REST API's client, but some examples include scripts loaded in web pages, handheld games, and business-critical applications running on server farms. REST APIs are designed to suit the needs of their client programs, whatever those needs may be.

This chapter provides a set of REST API design principles to address common client concerns. It concludes with a few rules to address the special needs of browser-based JavaScript clients.

Versioning

A REST API is composed of an assembly of interlinked resources: its resource model. The version of each resource is conveyed through its representational form and state.

Rule: New URIs should be used to introduce new concepts

A resource is a semantic model, like a *thought* about a *thing*. A resource's representational form and state may change over time but the identifier must consistently address the same *thought*, which no other URI can identify. Furthermore, every character in a resource's URI contributes to its identity. Therefore the *version* of a REST API, or any of its resources, typically should not be signified in a URI. For example, including a version indicator, like *v2*, in a URI conveys that the *concept* itself has multiple versions, which is usually not the intent.

A URI identifies a resource, independent of the version of its representational form and state. REST APIs should maintain a consistent mapping of its URIs to its conceptually constant resources. A REST API should introduce a new URI only if it intends to expose a new concept.

Rule: Schemas should be used to manage representational form versions

As discussed earlier in "Media Type Schema Versioning" on page 43, the version of the form of a REST API's resource representations is managed through versioned schema documents. Clients use media type negotiation to bind to the representational forms that best suit their needs.

Adding fields and links to new schema versions is a great way to introduce new features to a REST API without impacting backward compatibility.

Rule: Entity tags should be used to manage representational state versions

The section "Rule: ETag should be used in responses" on page 36 covered the use of ETag HTTP header to convey the version of a resource's representational state. The entity tag values associated with each individual resource are a REST API's most fine-grained versioning system.

Security

Many REST APIs expose resources that are associated with a specific client and/or user. For example, a REST API's documents may contain private information and its controllers may expose operations intended to be executed by a restricted audience.

The rules in this section address the protection of a REST API's sensitive resources.

Rule: OAuth may be used to protect resources

OAuth (Open Authorization) is an open standard that provides secure authorization using a consistent approach for all clients. It is best known for its role in allowing users to share their private resources, such as photos or contact lists, stored on one web site with another site without having to disclose their confidential username or password.

OAuth is described as an "open standard" because the protocol specification is not owned or controlled by any corporation, but rather, is managed by the OAuth Working Group within the IETF. The WG is comprised of individuals from Google, Microsoft, Facebook, Twitter, Yahoo, and other leading Internet companies.

OAuth is an HTTP-based authorization protocol that enables the protection of resources. The OAuth protocol's flow is summarized in the steps below:

1. A client obtains the *artifacts* needed to interact with a REST API's protected resources. Note that with respect to the character of these artifacts and how they are obtained, there are some significant differences between versions of the OAuth protocol specification.

2. Using the artifacts that it obtained in Step 1, the client requests an interaction with a REST API's protected resource.

3. The REST API, or an intermediary acting on its behalf, validates the client request's OAuth-based authorization information. Note that there are some significant differences in the validation process as detailed by the OAuth 1.0[*] and 2.0[†] specifications.

4. If the validation check succeeds, the REST API allows the client's interaction with the protected resource to proceed.

Architecturally, the OAuth protocol helps a REST API address security concerns in a manner that is complementary to the resource-centric and stateless nature of its interactions with clients.

Rule: API management solutions may be used to protect resources

An API reverse proxy is a relatively new type of network-based intermediary that may be used to secure a REST API's resources. API management solution vendors, such as Apigee[‡] and Mashery,[§] offer reverse proxy-based services to address many of the cross-cutting concerns related to producing, and consuming, high-quality REST APIs. These vendor solutions offer support for OAuth and other security protocols right out of the box.

Response Representation Composition

The needs of a REST API's clients can evolve over time. As new features are added, a client may require new resources from its supporting REST API. At times, the client's changes may be less drastic, requiring an API's existing resources be modeled in a slightly different way. Many REST APIs support multiple client *types*, with varying needs that must be accommodated.

A REST API can show respect for its clients by offering them a measure of control over the composition of its response representations. Following the rules presented in this section will enable clients to *tune* responses to meet their needs, while allowing the REST API to maintain a consistent resource model design.

---

[*] The OAuth 1.0 Protocol, *http://tools.ietf.org/html/rfc5849*

[†] The OAuth 2.0 Authorization Protocol, *http://tools.ietf.org/html/draft-ietf-oauth-v2*

[‡] *http//www.apigee.com*

[§] *http//www.mashery.com*

Rule: The query component of a URI should be used to support partial responses

A resource's current state is represented by a set of fields and links, as detailed in Chapter 5. There may be times when a REST API offers a resource state model that includes a bit more data than the client wishes to receive. In order to save on bandwidth, and possibly accelerate the overall interaction, a REST API's client can use the query component to trim response data with the `fields` parameter.

The `fields` query parameter allows clients to request only the resource state information that it deems relevant for its particular use case. The REST API must parse the request's query parameter's *inclusion list* and return a partial response. The following example request uses the `fields` query parameter to request that a specific subset of data be returned for the identified *student* document:

```
# Request
GET /students/morgan?fields=(firstName, birthDate) HTTP/1.1   ❶
Host: api.college.restapi.org

# Response
HTTP/1.1 200 OK
Content-Type: application/wrml;
              format="http://api.formats.wrml.org/application/json";
              schema="http://api.schemas.wrml.org/college/Student";
              fields="(birthDate, firstName)"   ❷

{
    "firstName" : "Morgan",   ❸
    "birthDate" : "1992-07-31"
}
```

❶ The request includes the `fields` parameter, which specifies the list of fields that should be included in the response's representation.

❷ When the `fields` query parameter is used to define an inclusion list, the media type must specify a parameter, also named `fields`, which canonicalizes the response's field list in case-insensitive, alphabetical order.

❸ The partial response contains only the `firstName` and `birthDate` fields.

In the example above, the `fields` query parameter syntax indicated that the client wished to obtain the current state of two specific fields. However, sometimes it may be more convenient for the client to designate the resource state fields that it does *not* want to receive. For example, a client may ask an API to exclude an indicated set of fields whose values are known to be sizable and unused.

The example request below demonstrates how the `fields` query parameter can be used to specify a set of fields that are unwanted:

```
# Request
GET /students/morgan?fields=!(address,schedule!(wednesday, friday))  HTTP/1.1   ❶
Host: api.college.restapi.org
```

```
# Response
HTTP/1.1 200 OK
Content-Type: application/wrml;
            format="http://api.formats.wrml.org/application/json";
            schema="http://api.schemas.wrml.org/college/Student";
            fields="!(address, schedule!(friday, wednesday))"  ❷

{
    "firstName" : "Morgan",  ❸
    "birthDate" : "1992-07-31",
    "schedule"  : {
        "monday" : {
            "links" : {
                "firstClass" : {
                    "href" : "http://api.college.restapi.org/classes/math-202",
                    "rel"  : "http://api.relations.wrml.org/college/firstClass"
                },

                # Daily schedule's other links...
            }
        },

        # Schedule's other fields (except friday and wednesday)...
    },

    # Student's other fields (except address)...

    "links" : {
        # Student's links...
    }
}
```

❶ The exclamation point character (!), which precedes the parenthetically enclosed and comma-separated names, declares a field *exclusion list*.

❷ When the `fields` query parameter is used to define an exclusion list, it alters the structure of the form away from its schema's definition; thus it needs to equivalently alter the `Content-Type` header's value. The media type must specify a `fields` parameter that lists the response's excluded fields in case-insensitive, alphabetical order.

❸ The REST API's partial response should then include all of the state representation's fields, except those indicated in the exclusion list.

In this example, the `schedule` field's value is an object with its own set of fields. The `schedule` field, which is named within the outer exclusion list, includes a nested exclusion list that omits the `wednesday` and `friday` fields.

 Clients should be encouraged to programmatically consult the resource's media type's schema to validate their field selections. See "Media Type Schema Design" on page 42 for more detail.

Rule: The query component of a URI should be used to embed linked resources

In his "Commentary on Web Architecture," Tim Berners-Lee pointed out that there are two types of links:

> Basic HTML has three ways of linking to other material on the web: the hypertext link from an anchor (HTML "A" element), the general link with no specific source anchor within the document (HTML "LINK" element), and embedded objects and images (IMG and OBJECT). Let's call A and LINK "normal" links, as they are visible to the user as a traversal between two documents. We'll call the thing between a document and an embedded image or object or subdocument "embedding" links.
>
> —Tim Berners-Lee *http://www.w3.org/DesignIssues/LinkLaw*

REST API's should allow individual client requests to control which linked resources should remain "normal" and which ones should become "embedded." This request-time composition approach allows a REST API to present a consistent, fine-grained resource model while empowering its clients to create facades that better match their individual use cases.

Consider the representation below:

```
{
    "firstName" : "Morgan",
    "birthDate" : "1992-07-31",

    # Other fields...

    "links" : {
        "self" : {
            "href" : "http://api.college.restapi.org/students/morgan",
            "rel"  : "http://api.relations.wrml.org/common/self"
        },
        "favoriteClass" : {
            "href" : "http://api.college.restapi.org/classes/japn-301",
            "rel"  : "http://api.relations.wrml.org/college/favoriteClass"
        },

        # Other links...
    }
}
```

Clients use the `embed` query parameter to identify the link relations that they wish to have included, as `fields`, directly in the response's representation. The following example request uses the `embed` query parameter to include the `favoriteClass` link as a field:

```
# Request
GET /students/morgan?embed=(favoriteClass) HTTP/1.1  ❶
Host: api.college.restapi.org

# Response
HTTP/1.1 200 OK
```

```
Content-Type: application/wrml;
             format="http://api.formats.wrml.org/application/json";
             schema="http://api.schemas.wrml.org/college/Student";
             embed="(favoriteClass)"  ❷

{
    "firstName" : "Morgan",
    "birthDate" : "1992-07-31",
    "favoriteClass" : {  ❸
        "id" : "japn-301",
        "name" : "Third-Year Japanese",
        "links" : {
            "self" : {
                "href" : "http://api.college.restapi.org/classes/japn-301",
                "rel"  : "http://api.relations.wrml.org/common/self"
            }
        }
    }

    # Other fields...

    "links" : {
        "self" : {
            "href" : "http://api.college.restapi.org/students/morgan",
            "rel"  : "http://api.relations.wrml.org/common/self"
        },

        ❹

        # Other links...
    }
}
```

❶ In this example the embed query parameter specifies a single link, favoriteClass, but it can be used to specify a list of links (like the fields parameter discussed in "Rule: The query component of a URI should be used to support partial responses" on page 74).

❷ When the embed query parameter is used, it alters the structure of the form away from its schema's definition, thus it needs to equivalently alter the Content-Type header's value. The media type must specify an embed parameter that lists the embedded links in case-insensitive, alphabetical order.

❸ The REST API has retrieved a representation of the linked favoriteClass resource and has embedded it as a field.

❹ The favoriteClass link is now gone, replaced by the embedded field.

> Note that embedding only works for link relations that use the GET method and support the exact same media type *format* as the referencing representation.

Processing Hypermedia

Chapter 5 introduced two hypermedia structures, *link* and *link relation*. These structures are designed to be easy for clients to process using a consistent algorithm. The flowchart in Figure 6-1 illustrates how a client should interact with a particular REST API response representation's link.

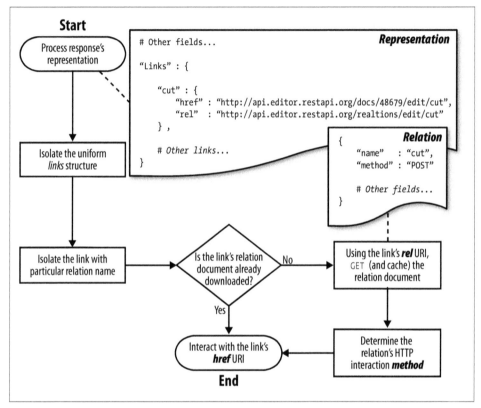

Figure 6-1. Hypermedia processing flowchart

As shown in the flowchart, the client's hypermedia processing routine starts by simply looking up the link using its relation's name. Then, in order to interact with the link using the appropriate HTTP request method, the client's code inspects the method field of the link's relation document resource. If the link's interaction allows or requires content to be submitted in the request message's body, then the link relation document would indicate the possible media type options via its requestTypes field.

JavaScript Clients

The modern web browser, with its ubiquity and ever-increasing power, is a natural platform for client applications. The JavaScript programming language facilitates the development of applications that are instantly available *everywhere*. JavaScript programs provide the interactive parts of web experiences. They make: applications dynamic, games playable, and advertisements noticeable.

The rules presented in this section apply to REST APIs that wish to support the growing number of JavaScript-based clients which are "sandboxed" by the web browser's *same origin policy*.‖ The same origin policy, which is also known as the *same domain policy*, restricts a browser-based JavaScript client from accessing resources from any web servers other than its code's own source. Web browsers enforce the same origin policy to prevent leaking of confidential user data. A resource's *origin* is defined# by its URI's scheme, host, and port components.

The following resources have the same origin:

```
http://restapi.org
http://restapi.org:80   ❶
http://restapi.org/js/my-mashup.js   ❷
```

❶ This URI is the same as the first one because 80 is HTTP's default port.

❷ This is the same as the others because the URI's path is not part of a resource's origin.

In contrast, each the following resources has a different origin.

```
http://restapi.org
https://restapi.org      ❶
http://www.restapi.org   ❷
http://restapi.org:8080  ❸
https://restapi.org:80
http://restapi.com
http://wrml.org
```

❶ The use of the *https* scheme makes this a different origin.

❷ The *www* subdomain identifies a different host, which is part of the resource's origin.

❸ 8080 and 80 are two different ports.

Many JavaScript web applications dynamically integrate a variety of content and services from several APIs; each one with a different scheme, host, or port. With their tendency to cleverly combine data from more than one origin, these clients are commonly known as *mashups*. Today, there are a few different ways that REST APIs can provide multi-origin access, namely *JSONP* and *CORS*, which are described by the rules of this section.

‖ *http://www.w3.org/Security/wiki/Same_Origin_Policy*

\#The Web origin concept, *http://tools.ietf.org/html/draft-ietf-websec-origin*

Rule: JSONP should be supported to provide multi-origin read access from JavaScript

The JSONP (JSON with Padding) request technique is a very useful *hack*. With a little bit of extra work done by both the client and the REST API, JSONP enables multi-origin read-only access from JavaScript.

The browser's built-in `XMLHttpRequest` component provides its JavaScript clients with HTTP client functionality.[*] The browser quirk that opens the door for JSONP is that, although `XMLHttpRequest` is blocked from making requests to third-party hosts, there is *not* a similar restriction on HTML `script` elements. Leveraging this, the JSONP request technique adds a `<script src="…">` element to the browser's Document Object Model (DOM), with a REST API's URI as the `src` target. Therefore, for each new JSONP request, the client must dynamically add a new `script` tag into the HTML DOM, with the desired URI as the `src` attribute's value.

JavaScript clients indicate to the REST API that they desire a JSONP "wrapped" response by adding a `callback` query parameter to the *src* attribute's URI value. Once the `script` element is injected into the DOM, it is evaluated and the `src` URI is retrieved, via HTTP `GET`, from the API.

Seeing the added `callback` query parameter, the REST API should return the JSON response data wrapped in the requested callback function. The calling of the JavaScript client's callback function is the "padding" wrapped around the API's normal JSON formatted response representation. Finally, the browser's JavaScript engine will execute the response, which results in the specified callback function being invoked with the response's JSON data passed in as a parameter.

JSONP works on both modern and legacy browsers, but due to its `script` element injection nature, it is limited to making `GET` requests.

Below is an example of the JSONP request technique. The example starts with the JavaScript client code, which uses the popular jQuery[†] library to call a REST API that supports JSONP:

```
var getPlayer = function(uri, successCallback) { ❶
    $.ajax({ ❷
        url: uri,
        success: successCallback,
        dataType: 'jsonp'
    });
};

var showPlayerFullName = function(player) { ❸
    alert(player.firstName + " " + player.lastName);
};
```

---

[*] http://www.w3.org/TR/XMLHttpRequest

[†] http://www.jquery.com

```
getPlayer("http://api.soccer.restapi.org/players/1421", showPlayerFullName);  ❹
```

❶ JavaScript declaration of a **getPlayer** function that expects two parameters: a URI string and the name of a callback function.

❷ Calls the jQuery library's **ajax** function; passing the URI and callback function name, along with a flag that tells the function to use the JSONP pattern.

❸ JavaScript declaration of a **showPlayerFullName** function that expects a **Player** object and pops up a simple message box with text that displays the player's full name. This is the example's callback function.

❹ Calls the **getPlayer** function; passing a URI that identifies a REST API's player resource (which has been hardcoded to simplify this illustration). The function's second parameter names the **showPlayerFullName** callback function.

In this example, the **getPlayer** function uses the jQuery AJAX‡ library's JSONP support to handle the **script** element injection and the addition of the **callback** query parameter to the end of the URI.

This example's associated HTTP request and response details are shown below:

```
# For brevity's sake, some headers, fields, and links have been
# omitted from this example.

# Request
GET /players/1421?callback=showPlayerFullName HTTP/1.1  ❶
Host: api.soccer.restapi.org

# Response
HTTP/1.1 200 OK
Content-Type: application/javascript  ❷

showPlayerFullName(  ❸
    {
        "firstName" : "Kasey",
        "lastName" : "Keller",
        "number" : 18,
        "birthDate" : "1969-11-29",

        "links" : {
            "self" : {
              "href" : "http://api.soccer.restapi.org/players/1421",
              "rel"  : "http://api.relations.wrml.org/common/self"
            }
        }
    }
);
```

❶ Note that the jQuery library has added the **callback** query parameter to the specified URI.

‡ AJAX is a popular acronym that stands for "Asynchronous JavaScript and XML."

❷ The REST API should set the `Content-Type` header of JSONP responses to `application/javascript` to indicate that the body format is now JavaScript rather than `application/json` (or some other application-specific media type).

❸ The REST API's response message body has wrapped the standard player resource's JSON structure with a *call* to the client's `showPlayerFullName` JavaScript function.

Finally, when the browser receives the response from the GET request it used to fetch the injected script tag's `src` URI, it *executes* the client's `showPlayerFullName` JavaScript function call. The end result of this example is that the browser shows an alert message box with the text "Kasey Keller".

In summary, REST APIs enable JSONP client requests by supporting an optional `call back` query parameter. If the parameter is present in a request, the API should wrap its normal JSON response body's data in a JavaScript function call with the `callback` query parameter's value as the function's name.

Rule: CORS should be supported to provide multi-origin read/write access from JavaScript

Cross-Origin Resource Sharing[§] (CORS) is the W3C's proposed approach to standardize cross-origin requests from the browser. CORS is an alternative to JSONP (see "Rule: JSONP should be supported to provide multi-origin read access from Java-Script" on page 80) that supports all request methods. The CORS approach enhances `XMLHttpRequest`, the browser's built-in HTTP client, to natively support cross-origin requests.

For request methods other than: GET, HEAD, and POST; CORS defines a *preflight* request interaction. The preflight request occurs "behind-the-scenes" between a CORS-compliant browser and server, in advance of the JavaScript client's *actual request* to access a cross-origin resource. REST APIs may use the CORS-proposed `Access-Control-Allow-Origin` HTTP header to list the set of origins that are permitted cross-origin access to its resources. Most modern browsers support CORS by sending special HTTP request headers such as `Origin` and `Access-Control-Request-Method`. The `Origin` header value identifies the requesting JavaScript client's scheme/host/port source location. The `Access-Control-Request-Method` header value is sent in the CORS preflight request to indicate which HTTP method will be used in the client's actual request.

The following JavaScript function presents the typical approach to dealing with the various browsers' nonstandard implementations of the proposed CORS standard:

```
function createCORSRequest(method, url) {
    var xhr = new XMLHttpRequest();
    if ("withCredentials" in xhr) {  ❶
        xhr.open(method, url, true);
```

§ *http://www.w3.org/TR/cors*

```
    }
    else if (typeof XDomainRequest != "undefined") { ❷
        xhr = new XDomainRequest();
        xhr.open(method, url);
    }
    else {
        xhr = null; ❸
    }
    return xhr;
}
```

❶ Idiomatic code that tests the browser's CORS support.

❷ Microsoft's Internet Explorer 8 browser requires JavaScript clients to use the special XDomainRequest object for cross-domain requests.‖

❸ Returns *null* if the browser does not support CORS.

Recap

This chapter presented REST API design tips that help address client concerns. Table 6-1 summarizes the terms that were introduced.

Table 6-1. Vocabulary review

Term	Description
API reverse proxy	A network-based intermediary that addresses many of the cross-cutting concerns associated with REST APIs.
Cross-Origin Resource Sharing (CORS)	The W3C's proposed approach to standardize cross-origin requests from the browser.
Document Object Model (DOM)	A browser-based, client-side API that allows JavaScript code to interact with the elemental structure loaded in the browser's memory.
Embedded link	A related resource that is retrieved and integrated into a referencing resource as a field.
Exclusion list	A set of fields to be omitted from a message body that contains a representation.
Inclusion list	The complete set of fields that a client expects to find within a message body that contains a representation.
JSONP	Uses DOM scripting to support cross-origin GET requests from JavaScript.
Mashup	A client that intertwines information and features that originate from a variety of unrelated resources.
OAuth	An open standard authorization protocol that may be used to protect a REST API's resources.
Partial response	The result of a client-controlled winnowing of a message body that contains a representation.
Same origin policy	Restricts a browser-based JavaScript client from accessing resources from any web servers other than its code's own source.

‖ *http://msdn.microsoft.com/en-us/library/cc288060(v=vs.85).aspx*

## CHAPTER 7

Final Thoughts

State of the Art

Today, implementing our REST API designs is harder than it ought to be. The tools and frameworks that aim to support REST API developers have room for improvement. Many of the programming language-centric REST API development frameworks were originally created to help build web applications. These frameworks seem to suggest that REST APIs are similar enough to web applications that they should be cast from the same mold.

By repurposing the web application's *controller* paradigm, many of today's frameworks provide support for using URI templates to route inbound client requests to *handler-style* methods or functions. In recognition of the fact that developers don't want to code web page templates to format their REST API's data, most of the frameworks offer built-in XML and JSON-based serialization and deserialization of the server's objects to and from an HTTP message's body.

Today, there is no unanimous *winner* among the various REST API development framework candidates. The selection amounts to personal (or organizational) preference of programming language and platform.

Unfortunately, most of the current REST API development frameworks lack direct support for:

- Natural separation of the resource model from the server's implementation model
- Uniform, cross-format hypermedia structures
- Automated HATEOAS; based on current state, determining which links should be provided in a response
- Media type schema validation and versioning
- Both *partial* and *dynamically composed* response bodies
- Integration with client identification and entitlement authority
- Multi-origin resource sharing with JSONP and CORS

The lack of framework support for many core features has left REST API developers with a difficult choice: either omit features or code them yourself. Unsatisfied with these options, many developers have turned to API management solutions, as discussed in "Rule: API management solutions may be used to protect resources" on page 73, to provide some of these expected features. These solutions are helpful, but they can quickly become *too* helpful. Reliance on API management solutions to provide important (yet nonstandard) REST API features may lead an organization to become locked into a specific vendor's implementation. The Web's network-based intermediaries must be transparent to clients and servers, which also means they should be easily *swappable*.

Migrating from one vendor's API management solution to another's, or switching development frameworks, requires a degree of REST API design standardization that has yet to be achieved.

Uniform Implementation

Coding a REST API has never felt right to me. I believe that REST APIs should be designed and configured, but not *coded*. To that end, I've conceived of an alternative approach to REST API implementation that is founded on the WRML conceptual framework's architectural principles. These principles, summarized below, align with the REST API design methodology presented as this book's rules.

Principle: REST API designs differ more than necessary

REST APIs, while becoming ubiquitous, are far from uniformly designed. The *RESTfulness* of APIs continues to be debated by those that create and consume them. In the absence of standards, REST API designers are free to innovate and explore new concepts, which is a good thing. However, when REST API designs eventually converge on a set of common patterns that address each one of the cross-cutting concerns, developers will benefit from the uniformity.

If history is any indication, this uniformity will most likely be driven by a *pragmatic* and detailed standard for REST API design. This book's rule-based expression of a REST API's expected behavior is a good indication that a more detailed specification can eventually be written to standardize a common approach. Then, this standard can be leveraged to develop reusable frameworks and libraries for clients, servers, and network-based intermediaries.

For interoperability's sake, a REST API design standard must be *neutral* with respect to programming languages and representation formats. As highlighted in the design of WRML's media type, the *schema* can universally describe a program's data structure without binding it to any specific expression format. The abstract nature of schemas allow them to be consumed by clients and servers written in different programming languages. Furthermore, the WRML-based schemas and their associated link relations are designed to be shared and leveraged by a variety of REST APIs, which, along with decentralized Web-based hosting, can further their reusabilty across organizational boundaries.

Of equal importance is the governance of such a standardized approach to REST API design. In its lively 20 year history, the Web has withstood a few notable attempts to own or control one of its important parts. The Web has weathered the years of ad-hoc standardization by browser vendors. More recently, the Web rebelled against various vendor attempts to own its image, animation, and video formats. Similarly, attempts to standardize the design and implementation of REST APIs, either in part or as a whole, will succeed or fail based on the open and nonproprietary governance of their ideas and source code.

Principle: A REST API should be designed, not coded

Coding a REST API typically means programming an interface that exposes a backend system's resources to Web-aware clients. In practice, this task varies slightly, depending on the chosen programming language and framework. However, the core job remains the same: write code that handles HTTP-level details and translates a backend system's data model into a Web-oriented resource model. Some of this code most certainly needs to be written on a per-API basis, specifically the portion that directly communicates with the backend system or data store. However, a uniform REST API layer can be developed to replace the boilerplate and bookkeeping code found in many current implementations.

In WRML's conceptual architecture, the uniform REST API layer is a configuration-driven engine that resides within a *web resource server*. As shown in Figure 7-1, the web resource server accepts client requests and delegates them to its core engine. The engine's design may ultimately be standardized so that it can be consistently implemented for each web server-based programming framework that wishes to embrace its architectural style.

The engine takes a step-oriented approach to request handling, with each step and the order of all steps specified through configuration. Common steps are used to handle resource template routing, media type negotiation, client authorization, error handling, multi-origin support, and other core REST API features. When each step is executed, it is passed the *context* of the request, which is a thread-local associative array that accumulates request processing information as each step is executed. Ultimately, the engine's algorithm reaches a point where it *connects* to the backend system to resolve the requested resource.

Through a minimalistic interface, the engine asks the backend system to *fill in* a generic form-oriented structure that is an *instance* of the client-negotiated media type's schema. In other words, the backend system is handed a form-like "data template" that it must fill in with the current state information. In addition to filling in the schema-specific form field's current values, the backend system must also provide a list of zero or more

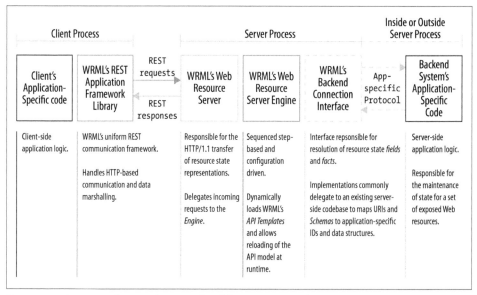

Client Process			Server Process			Inside or Outside Server Process
Client's Application-Specific code	WRML's REST Application Framework Library	REST requests / REST responses	WRML's Web Resource Server	WRML's Web Resource Server Engine	WRML's Backend Connection Interface / App-specific Protocol	Backend System's Application-Specific Code
Client-side application logic.	WRML's uniform REST communication framework. Handles HTTP-based communication and data marshalling.		Responsible for the HTTP/1.1 transfer of resource state representations. Delegates incoming requests to the *Engine*.	Sequenced step-based and configuration driven. Dynamically loads WRML's *API Templates* and allows reloading of the API model at runtime.	Interface repsonsible for resolution of resource state *fields* and *facts*. Implementations commonly delegate to an existing server-side codebase to maps URIs and *Schemas* to application-specific IDs and data structures.	Server-side application logic. Responsible for the maintenance of state for a set of exposed Web resources.

Figure 7-1. WRML application framework—delivery system architecture

state facts that are currently *true* about the requested resource. From here, the engine's HATEOAS calculator evaluates the selected schema's *link formulas* using the backend system's provided state facts as operands. Once the form is completely filled in, with both fields and links, the engine adds it to the request's context and executes the remaining response-oriented steps.

Principle: Programmers and their organizations benefit from consistency

Web developers have benefited from the uniformity, or at least near-uniformity, of the browser's implementation of HTML's element-based structure, CSS's presentation rules, and the DOM-oriented JavaScript API. Historically, HTML pages, with their fields and links, have been the Web's primary *type system*. Servers generate web pages and clients submit their forms. Without this consistency, there would be no singular and open Web as we know it today.

On today's server-side, in the realm of REST APIs, its a bit like the pioneering days of America's Wild West: not *completely* lawless, but nearly so. The inconsistency of REST API designs hinders the transition of web applications to their next logical architecture, where web servers provide structured data and leave the presentation responsibilities to their enriched clients. In this architecture, web applications use JavaScript to render *screens* in the browser and interact with REST APIs that provide consistently formed representations. This approach reduces a server's workload by shifting some of the processing duty to its users' client devices, which have fast and powerful CPUs. In short, this architecture requires less server-side computational capacity, which reduces the total cost of operation.

The WRML architectural approach to REST API implementation moves the traditional idea of web page templates toward the back of the system, as close as possible to its data source. A benefit of this methodology is that it reuses the exact same schema structures as *templates* for the backend to fill in and as *contracts* for clients to consume and introspect. In a world of multi-device clients with different formatting needs, this architecture frees up server developers to focus on advancing the web application's business logic in their backend systems, instead of worrying about all of the REST API design rules presented in this book.

With a baseline level of server interface uniformity, new client-side frameworks can be developed to abstract away the mundane code related to HTTP-based communication and data marshalling. Of course, underneath the covers, these client-server interactions are REST-based, so we can be sure that the Web will continue to function as intended.

Principle: A REST API should be created using a GUI tool

With widespread acceptance of a common set of rules, I believe that we can advance a shared REST API design methodology and begin to fashion a uniformly programmable Web. However, uniform REST API design is not the ultimate goal—it is only a means to an end. The greatest benefit of a standardized design and implementation methodology is the availability of helpful frameworks and tools that increase developer productivity. For example, the WRML conceptual architecture can be leveraged to develop tools that allow users to graphically design REST APIs. See Figure 7-2 for a set of mockups that depict a conceptual REST API design tool's graphical user interface.

Behind the scenes, the tool can generate the structures that WRML's web resource server engine reads as configuration data whenever it loads a running REST API instance. In fact, this REST API configuration data may be loaded and dynamically reloaded, without restarting the web resource server. This nimble approach to REST API design and development is shown in Figure 7-3.

The web resource server engine's configuration data consists of a small set of core constructs, which are summarized below:

API template
> A named REST API containing a list of resource templates, a list of schemas, and a list of "global" API-level state facts.

Resource template
> A resource template is a path segment within a REST API's hierarchical resource model. It has an associated URI template and set of possible schemas that client's may bind to, at request time, by using media type negotiation. The schemas that are assigned to a resource template must extend one of the four base schemas associated with the resource archetypes: `Document`, `Collection`, `Store`, and `Controller`.

Figure 7-2. Mockup showing a REST API design tool

Schema

Schemas are like classes or tables: they are a web application's structured types. They allow forms (*instances* consisting of fields and links) to be molded in their image and used to carry the state of a resource.

Format

Formats, like HTML, XML, and JSON, are often used on their own to declare the type associated with the content of a message's body. WRML elevates formats to first-class structures that can provide links to downloadable code to help programs exchange their encoded data.

Link relation

A link relation is a concept borrowed from HTML that adds semantics to links. WRML expands on the idea by also documenting a link's acceptable input media types and possible output media types.

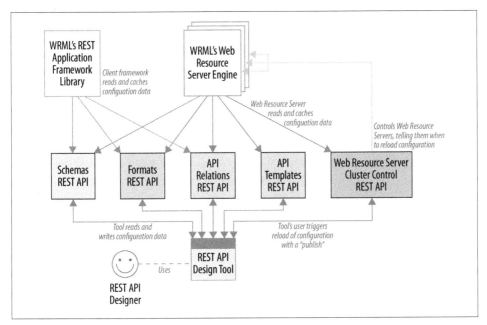

Figure 7-3. WRML REST API configuration architecture

Recap

The modern tools and frameworks supporting REST API development are, in a word, *underwhelming*. However, by adopting a common REST API design methodology, we can advance the state of the art. Then, we will be able to spend less time *coding* programmatic interfaces and focus our efforts on writing web application code: the stuff that really matters.

My First REST API

I designed my first REST API shortly after joining Starwave in June of 1997.

While working as a programmer in the Sports Engineering group, I was tasked with developing a new Java applet for a web page on the *NASCAR Online* website. The *Race Tracker* applet was designed to display the status of the lead cars during a live race event. Once loaded in the user's web browser, the applet needed to continually fetch the current race status data from a server hosted by Starwave. At that time, Java applets could use either a raw socket or HTTP to access data on remote servers. However, if the applet's requests needed to cross over the Internet, or even just pass through firewalls, HTTP was the only real option.[*] In other words, the Java applet needed to talk to a Web API.

By the time I joined the company, the foundations for delivering this type of data over the Web had already been established by Starwave's team of talented software engineers. Leveraging a proprietary, Java 1.1-based, automated, real-time wire feed processing and publishing system known as "Bulldog," the server side of my task was to create a new web page template that would access and format the race data to be displayed by the applet. For a given live race event, Bulldog pulled in the data from a wire feed, created Java objects based on the data, then *published* the objects through my new template to constantly update a plain text file hosted on a standard web server.

These text files, each one containing the current state of a given live race event, were the Web API's *resources*. And, as a result of the Bulldog Web publishing process, each resource was uniquely identified with its own URI. The applet periodically requested a representation of a resource, via HTTP GET, to download and display the current state of a given race. I designed the race status resource representation by formatting each data element as a *row* on its own line and used the pipe (|) character to delimit each attribute (or *column*). For example:

```
1|1234|Ricky Bobby|26|http://hostname:port/images/drivers/1234.jpg|...
```

---

[*] This constraint placed on applet-to-server communication was the "original browser sandbox."

Along with the other data, the representation also included hyperlinks, which occupied consistent attribute *cells* (i.e., the slot between the fourth and fifth pipe character). The links enabled the applet to download and display images of the race car's sponsor logo and the driver's face.

The design of the Race Tracker applet's Web API certainly did not abide by all of the rules outlined in this book. However, it did make use of URIs, HTTP, and representations with hypermedia. And this is the point: REST describes the way the Web *already works*. REST isn't an invention; it is a prescription. By applying the hallmarks of the Web to the design of APIs, it can be quite natural to employ the REST architectural style.

About the Author

Mark Massé resides in Seattle, where he is a Senior Director of Engineering at ESPN. In his spare time, Mark enjoys spending time with family and friends, playing soccer and cheering on the Seattle Sounders, and talking about the video games that he wishes he had time to play. Most of all, Mark loves to hang out with Shawna.

Get even more for your money.

Join the O'Reilly Community, and register the O'Reilly books you own. It's free, and you'll get:

- $4.99 ebook upgrade offer
- 40% upgrade offer on O'Reilly print books
- Membership discounts on books and events
- Free lifetime updates to ebooks and videos
- Multiple ebook formats, DRM FREE
- Participation in the O'Reilly community
- Newsletters
- Account management
- 100% Satisfaction Guarantee

Signing up is easy:

1. **Go to: oreilly.com/go/register**
2. **Create an O'Reilly login.**
3. **Provide your address.**
4. **Register your books.**

Note: English-language books only

To order books online:
oreilly.com/store

For questions about products or an order:
orders@oreilly.com

To sign up to get topic-specific email announcements and/or news about upcoming books, conferences, special offers, and new technologies:
elists@oreilly.com

For technical questions about book content:
booktech@oreilly.com

To submit new book proposals to our editors:
proposals@oreilly.com

O'Reilly books are available in multiple DRM-free ebook formats. For more information:
oreilly.com/ebooks

Spreading the knowledge of innovators   oreilly.com

The information you need, when and where you need it.

With Safari Books Online, you can:

Access the contents of thousands of technology and business books

- Quickly search over 7000 books and certification guides
- Download whole books or chapters in PDF format, at no extra cost, to print or read on the go
- Copy and paste code
- Save up to 35% on O'Reilly print books
- **New!** Access mobile-friendly books directly from cell phones and mobile devices

Stay up-to-date on emerging topics before the books are published

- Get on-demand access to evolving manuscripts.
- Interact directly with authors of upcoming books

Explore thousands of hours of video on technology and design topics

- Learn from expert video tutorials
- Watch and replay recorded conference sessions

Milton Keynes UK
Ingram Content Group UK Ltd.
UKHW050359220924
448614UK00002BA/12